M000227157

THE HIGHEST APPLE

SAPPHO AND THE LESBIAN POETIC TRADITION

JUDY GRAHN

A Sapphic Classic from
Sinister Wisdom

The Highest Apple: Sappho and the Lesbian Poetic Tradition ©
2023 by Judy Grahn. All rights reserved.

Foreword © 2021 by Alyse Knorr. All rights reserved.
Editor's Note © by Alicia Mountain. All rights reserved.
Responses copyright © 2023 by individual authors.
All rights reserved.

Sinister Wisdom, Inc.
2333 McIntosh Road
Dover, FL 33527
sinisterwisdom@gmail.com
www.sinisterwisdom.org
Julie R. Enszer, Editor and Publisher

Designed by Nieves Guerra
Edited by Alyse Knorr and Alicia Mountain
Transcription by Indie Beare
Copyedit by Amy Haejung
Proofread by Sidney Schmidt

Cover design by Nieves Guerra

First edition, November 2023

ISBN-13: 978-1-944981-65-5

Printed in the U.S.

To All Lovers

TABLE OF CONTENTS

FOREWORD
ALYSE KNORR

I first encountered Judy Grahn's work in 2009, in the excellent compendium *The Judy Grahn Reader*, an anthology that included selections of Grahn's poetry, fiction, verse drama, and cultural theory. Reading Grahn was a spiritual experience for me. I read her when I needed her most: when I was newly coming out as a lesbian during my MFA program and searching for myself anywhere in the canon. As Grahn explains in *The Highest Apple*, I was "floundering on the rocks of alienation from [my] own culture, [my] own center" (36); I had not yet been exposed to the poetry of my people. Having grown up in the Deep South, in a conservative religious environment, I had also internalized a tremendous amount of shame about my sexuality. I feared writing love poems with "she/her" pronouns and flinched when I heard other lesbians identify with the word "dyke," which sounded only like a slur to me. But Grahn traced the etymology of the word "bull-dyke" back to Boudica, a Celtic warrior queen and high priestess, in her essay "Butches, Bulldags, and the Queen of Bulldikery." "Bull-dyke," Grahn wrote, meant "altar of the people's power." Dykes were—are—warrior women.

I remember reading that passage and needing to come up for air. I was sitting in the kitchen of a house I shared with three male roommates. The afternoon sun illuminated one half of the book while the other remained in shadow. I felt like a superhero, with newfound power pulsing through my veins where once lived only shame.

For her own generation of LGBTQIA (lesbian, gay, bisexual, transgender, queer, intersex, asexual) poets and for those that have followed hers, Grahn has offered us a bounty of gifts. The gifts of courage and inspiration—necessary tools in the continual project of self-liberation. The gifts of our history, our cultural lineage, and our legacy, which the hetero/cisnormative canon has sought to erase. And the gifts of foreparents with roots stretching back to ancient times—to a small, light-filled island and a woman named Sappho who recognized all that is erotic in the sacred and all that is sacred in the erotic. Grahn extends to her readers the revolutionary idea that women matter, that LGBTQIA people matter. She has taught me how to maintain faith in the power of poetry through her steadfast belief that poetry can save lives, offer hope, and motivate people to change their lives for the better. Throughout the activist movements of the 1960s and 1970s, including feminism, civil rights, gay liberation, and beyond, Grahn wrote poetry, epics, verse dramas, fiction, and cultural studies. Her versatility and the expanse of her mind are staggering. Equally impressive are the inspiring honesty, authenticity, and courage with which she has lived her life.

Grahn's name derives from the Biblical character Judith, a Jewish woman who defended her community by infiltrating the enemy's camp and beheading their leader. It's a fitting moniker; Grahn first developed a warrior persona in childhood and adolescence, refusing to stay silent and turning homophobic insults into sources of power.

In *A Simple Revolution*, Grahn describes how, as a child, she liked to scale a seven-foot adobe wall in one sprinting barefoot leap and then survey her New Mexico town from her high vantage point (22)—a memory that clearly captures Grahn's daring strength and revolutionary vision. From a very early age, she committed herself to using her voice to fight for justice (23), and this fight would always be personal for her. Grahn was dishonorably discharged from the US Air Force due to her sexuality, denied housing and jobs, and beaten in public for dressing in masculine clothing. In 1965, she picketed the White House with the Mattachine Society, and in 1970 she began handprinting feminist poetry on a mimeograph machine she purchased.

One of Grahn's lifelong scholarly projects has been re-surfacing women's and LGBTQIA cultural histories and identifying the key roles that LGBTQIA people have played in their societies since ancient times. Grahn has rediscovered and re-written origin stories and mythologies centered around women and LGBT people, from the Mesopotamian priestess Enheduanna to the archaic Greek poet Sappho to Homer's Helen of Troy, all in a direct reaction to the censorship and erasure of these stories. By cobbling together information from anthropology, sociology, history, and poetry, Grahn has revised, reclaimed, and recovered women's and LGBTQIA stories in history, mythology, religion, and theories about humanity, challenging straightwashed, male-dominated stories that erase women and LGBTQIA people.

The Highest Apple represents a major culmination of these efforts. Through her careful analysis of poetry by Sappho, Amy Lowell, H.D., Gertrude Stein, Adrienne

Rich, Emily Dickinson, Audre Lorde, Paula Gunn Allen, Pat Parker, and Olga Broumas, as well as her fascinating history of lesbian communities, Grahn makes the case for a conscious tradition of lesbian writing that has been passed down for millennia. Her project is nothing less than to "re-mythologiz[e] our society" (224), presenting a women's version of history whose themes include autonomy, community, self-determination, the sacred erotic, and the will to survive. She establishes a lineage of lesbian writers in which lesbianism is a "place from which to speak and a lens through which to view our society at large"—one that is simultaneously "a central and an 'outsider' position from which to take a stance" (*Judy Grahn Reader*, 263). For Grahn, lesbian writing offers a new paradigm through which to view the world—a paradigm that values wholeness, integration, and community. Lesbian poetry, according to Grahn, connects us to the greater universe and offers unique mythic histories and models of community and relationships. The title of the book is drawn from a Sappho lyric about a ripe apple hanging so high up on the tree that the apple-pickers cannot reach it. In Grahn's imaginary, the apple signifies feminine powers, "the centrality of women to themselves, to each other and to their society" (50), kept safely out of reach of all oppressors.

Last September, I visited the Brooklyn Museum and saw Judy Chicago's *The Dinner Party* for the first time. The moment felt as deeply resonant as when I read Grahn's work for the first time: not surprising since both Grahn and Chicago were forged in the caldron of second-wave feminism. Here in this darkened room were three long banquet tables arranged in a triangle—an LGBTQIA symbol—with place settings for major historical women ranging from Sappho to Boudica to Sojourner Truth. Chicago, born almost exactly one year before Grahn and sharing her Biblical warrior name, offers in visual form what Grahn articulates in *The Highest Apple*—a communion of women linked across time, transcendent and apart from time, existing together in this ghostly room the way they exist in the minds of their living feminist descendants. Solidarity and community across generations is the promise offered by Judy Grahn, and in the dinner party of foremothers laid out in my own mind, Grahn sits in a valued seat at the table.

Reading Grahn in my kitchen thirteen years ago set me on a path that I have not left. As I have continued to further educate and liberate myself, closely studying the work of Audre Lorde, Pat Parker, Adrienne Rich, and Paula Gunn Allen, Grahn's *The Highest Apple* has provided me with a means to put these women into a family tree, an intentional tradition, a paradigm of lesbian thought continually expanding on itself and looking both ahead and behind. Works like *The Highest Apple* allow us to preserve the traditions of these poetic ancestors and push them forward forever.

"AFTER SAPPHO"
EDITOR'S NOTE
ALICIA MOUNTAIN

After Sappho, the others of us who are doing this
work sit mending tears in the fabrics of our myth also,
mending the tears in the tales Sappho said Love weaves,
mending the tapestries the old women storytellers once
made of the substance of a wholistic life. (160)

Judy Grahn's luminous text *The Highest Apple* is laden with insight. Once you've read this book through, flip the book open to any page and you'll still learn something new, understand a poem differently, find yourself in new territory. Grahn's essays are as ripe today as they were in 1985, when she first published *The Highest Apple*.

Now that my intimacy with the manuscript has deepened over the years of our editorial process, three of the simplest points that Grahn makes in the text continue to astonish me. First, Grahn writes, "I comprehend Sappho not as the 'first woman poet,' but as the last of that great era, and the only one to have some fragments survive" (43). As a literary scholar—and as a lesbian, too—I'd been trained to think of Sappho as the earliest forebearer of women in poetry and of Sapphic culture. I'd conceptualized my timeline with Sappho at the beginning because I thought we didn't have evidence of earlier women poets who'd laid the foundation for her. After reading *The Highest Apple*, I've come to realize that Sappho's extant work is the evidence of other women poets having laid a foundation so that this exceptionally gifted one from Lesbos found such renown and her songs so saturated her world that they have survived millennia. Of course, she (and we) had ancestors whose names have been lost.

Second, Sappho's poetry wasn't only for people like herself—lesbian poet women—it was for everyone in her world. Her poems are rich with imagery of religious rituals, men at war, the fruits of agriculture, parenthood, friendship, devotion in many configurations. I find myself delighted by the fact that Sappho wrote songs that straight people loved, too! While contemporary lesbian poetry may be treated as a subordinate literature, Sappho wasn't pigeonholed. This woman poet was a central and esteemed cultural figure in her world.

Third, Grahn writes, "what was her world like? Well, for one thing, it loved her" (44). I like to read that Grahn's question and answer out loud to really let it sink in. There was a world that loved a lesbian woman poet. When I say it out loud, it helps me believe that it could be real—that that world was already once real and could be so again. And though much of Sappho's vast body of work has not survived, the love her world had for her buoyed these fragments across vast and perilous time. I imagine her world must have loved me, also, thousands of years before my birth, having cherished her enough to keep her poem gifts that they might reach us, too.

There was an ancient poet named Sappho. She was a woman; she loved other women. She wasn't the first, she wasn't the last. She had company in this—she wasn't alone. Her writing was respected, admired, acclaimed, desired. She lived in a world that loved her. In 2023, these simple truths still bring me to my knees.

Throughout *The Highest Apple*, Grahn roots us in these principles. She examines a legacy of lesbian poets and poetics through the lens of Sappho, reminding us that these lineages are both vast and varied. Like Sappho, who "did not write of Lesbian love out of a negative comparison with heterosexual love, nor by contrasting its merits with anything else, nor by rationalizations," Grahn shows that this body of literature stands on its own (48). This is vital reading, not just for those interested in queer poetry or poetry by women, but for anyone concerned with subjectivity, the lyric, class and race in literature, myth-making, religion, the body, place, war, love . . . what I'll sum up by calling it *humanity*. Describing Sappho's central role in the world that loved her, Grahn explains:

> as a poet of her whole society she wrote stories illustrative of the doings of the gods, both masculine and feminine; wrote instructions for the appropriate behavior with respect to the gods and to human society; and she wrote wedding songs, as well as the overtly Lesbian love lyrics for which she is so famed and ill-famed . . . She used an internal, subjective voice in an objective, public manner. (98)

I lament that *The Highest Apple* has been out of print for some decades because we've needed this book. I'm convinced it has instructions for us to build a public world that loves lesbian woman poet subjectivities, by which I mean a world that loves anyone whose own subjectivity has been shaped in some way by lesbian people or women or poets, by which I mean a world that loves all of us, a world that loves you.

My co-editor, Alyse Knorr, and I approached this 2023 edition of *The Highest Apple* with the above notions guiding our editorial process. With the support of Julie Enszer and the *Sinister Wisdom* community, we worked to make the text available, resonant, and useful to a wide contemporary audience. Alyse and I made in-text revisions for clarity and contributed contextualizing footnotes to the manuscript. We were particularly thrilled to bring additional voices into conversation with *The Highest Apple*; the backmatter of this edition includes essays by Donika Kelly, Kim Shuck, Serena Chopra, Zoe Tuck, Saretta Morgan, and Khadijah Queen. These attuned responses enrich Grahn's text, midwifing this new edition into the world. I'm grateful to each of these contributors for their patience and brilliance. It has been an honor to develop this 2023 edition in collaboration with Judy Grahn herself. A new section in this edition, "Common Likeness, Common Difference," expands on Grahn's thinking about the poetry of Pat Parker. I admire her commitment to the evolution and reawakening of this text. I'm humbled by Judy's trust in me, Alyse, and Julie as we worked to bring the wisdom of *The Highest Apple* to new audiences.

Cultivating this project has been a great joy for me. It has brought me into closer, more bountiful communion with my literary ancestors, kith and kin. *The Highest Apple* reminds me that our historical pantheon—of poets, of women, of lesbian people—lives not in some distant past, nor on some unreachable celestial plane. Grahn's writing has given me permission to find abundance and warmth from even the most ancient sources. "I am going to assume," she writes, "that Sappho's Aphrodite was a goddess of intelligence, aesthetic balance and vision as well as of beauty and love. I believe this because there is no reason not to" (174). Where else can we assume beauty and love because there is no reason not to? Given that belief, what else becomes possible for us? Through Sappho, Grahn shows us the power of our own subjectivities. This lesbian, this woman, this poet:

> spoke of and to the gods, in her own personal voice, undistanced from them. In so doing, she spoke into the most collective consciousness of her culture without omitting her own personal consciousness. She spoke from a whole way of being, not an alienated, fragmented one; she spoke not as an outcast, but as someone at the very heart and center of her culture and of her times. (100)

Reader, I welcome you into *The Highest Apple* with the hope that you recognize something of yourself in these pages—someone not outcast, but at the heart and center of your world, undistanced from whatever you find holy.

INTRODUCTION

I could never have written this little book without first writing another, much longer one, of which this was originally to have been a chapter—a chapter on Sappho and the importance of poetry to Lesbians. The long book took ten years of research and effort and is called *Another Mother Tongue: Gay Words, Gay Worlds* (Boston: Beacon Press, 1984). By and large it is a Gay and Lesbian cultural history,[1] a complex exploration of stories, myths, and anthropological extrapolations concerning the possible meaning throughout history of certain words, phrases, and odd character traits commonly associated with Gayness. These include purple as the "Gay color," little finger rings, and names such as dyke, faggot, round, fairy, buggery, butch, queer, and the like.

Another Mother Tongue proposes that Gay people have a culture, that it cuts across class, race, gender, and even national and tribal categories. It proposes further that Gay people have functions in society that involve, and in fact require, Gay attributes. In short, it says that Gay culture is central to Gay people and that Gay people are central to their societies, even when they occupy a despised or underground position. I have used that idea in *The Highest Apple* also, with an additional proposition that women, too, have cultural heritage and central positions with regard to their societies. I have gone even further: I have supposed that even poets have important positions in society, whether acknowledged or not, and that Sappho is a prime example of such a poet and of such a central position.

Sappho gave us several traditions, among them a tradition of poets of Love, hardly the least of her contributions. Though I am, in *The Highest Apple*, treating a very special tradition that she also gave us, a Sapphic tradition of woman-bonding, I want to give all my thanks to a poetics department of love, the New College of California Poetics Program, who made the essays possible and who in every way carry on the tradition of poetry as a province of lovers—all lovers.

Lesbian culture may be seen as "marginal" by heterosexual culture and heterosexual definition, but surely Lesbian culture is central to Lesbians. Moreover, the work that comes from Lesbian culture, the special perspective, can be central to society as a whole. Especially if the women doing the work decide to give it that central direction. Both H.D.'s and Gertrude Stein's bodies of work are as central to the literature—and consequently the philosophical understandings—of the twentieth century as Emily Dickinson (and Walt Whitman) were for the nineteenth. Their work is not marginal, their lives were not marginal to their society, though perhaps they lived an extreme synthesis of the lives of most of their compatriots.

"Marginal" is a word that implies there is one world, and it is flat. At the edge is the "margin," occupied by those so-called "dangerous," powerless, and (poor) oppressed groups who have so vehemently defined themselves in the American mind in this twentieth century: Black, Gay, Lesbian, Jewish, Indigenous, "Third World," the elderly, Muslim, transgender, disabled, etc.

Fortunately, at the heart of these groups one finds an entirely different schema, a map virtually unrelated to the one held by the flat-world folks. I first saw this new way of looking very clearly when I was a young woman living with my first lover, Von, in the city of Washington, DC. Von taught physical education in the schools and was one of those teachers assigned to a number of schools, eight in all. She saw quite a bit of the city, which in 1963 and 1964 was rapidly altering its racial composition. Hopeful Black people pouring in from the South displaced much of Washington's white population, who fled in the face of their own racial fears and specters. Housing speculators fed their panic and the rising hopes of the Black community by doing "block-busting," deliberately terrorizing the white homeowners with visions of losing everything to low-class "ghetto dwellers," then re-selling the cheaply bought houses at inflated prices to incoming Black people. It was an ugly and often repeated American scene.

Von and I, like so many of our generation, were particularly sensitive and drawn to the situation of Black people, indeed of all the people defined as displaced, oppressed, "marginal." We identified with them because we came from poor and immigrant backgrounds in our own families, and because we ourselves, as Lesbians and as single women, were defined and treated as marginal, displaced, and oppressed.

Yet in the midst of this scenario, we spotted an entirely different one. We first heard the news on the radio; Washington's Black radio programming featured Elijah

Muhammad, a fiery speaker of the Black Nation of Islam. "Black Nation"—we had never heard of such a thing. We were frightened at first, and curious. Then our attention riveted to a more worldly version of Black separatism in the person of Malcom X. He was electrifying, and we followed the tumultuous history of the Black Muslims not only for what Black people were learning but also for what we were learning from him, about the essential importance of autonomy, self-determination, and community. I could tell that separatism and the centrality of a group of people to themselves were powerful social tools. The assassination of Malcolm X was the first of that series of killings that pierced the sixties with arrows of irrevocable determination and commitment. I remember experiencing his death as an understanding of the price of radical leadership, and that what we were—and are—involved in is a low-level ongoing war.

When five years later, in 1969, it was time for me to help form an organization that would further the development of Gay people, I joined with seven or eight other young women, several of whom had also experienced in one way or another the teachings of Malcolm X and who also, like me, had been strongly influenced by the Lesbian underground network of bars, cliques, and (in my case had published in) a Lesbian magazine, The Ladder. Several of our number were Jewish radical Lesbians, including my lover at the time, Wendy Cadden. Some were from the European folk "marginal culture" known variously as lower class, working class, white trash, or even middle class in sociological jargon. Some were Black, including poet Pat Parker as well as another outspoken woman who changed her Anglo-Saxon name to Amma. The organizations we proceeded to define and develop were Lesbian separatist, with a feminist and radical underbase. From the meetings grew all-women's households, institutions in and of themselves, that gave rise to others: to newspapers, to the first all-women's bookstore (A Woman's Place in Oakland, CA), to the first all-women's press (The Women's Press Collective). Meetings of all kinds took place in the house, such as the first meeting of what became the Lesbian Mothers Union, called by Black Lesbian organizer Pat Norman, and dozens of other meetings ranging from prison organizing to working for welfare rights, to anti-rape campaigns, to the editing of books and the promotion of artwork and literature.

Without our knowledge of the uses of separatism we might still have been straining to get a word in edgewise at the large meetings of Gay men with tangential, yet different, concerns, needs, and issues. Once we had our own concerns going, we found that plenty of people wanted to listen to us. We had a voice.

We had a voice of our own, and when it spoke the first words were through the poets. Masses of women came to those early readings and even more masses came later when it became "the thing to do." Fifteen years later— and long after the women musicians and songwriters, the dramatists, filmmakers, and comedians, political organizers and office holders have risen by the hundreds and thousands to fill in all the details of what we were barely outlining—"the movement" still keeps one ear to the ground to hear what else its poets may be telling. In every sense, we have been mediums. Involved in as much of our community as we could spare from our meditative work and the ever-present necessity of earning a living

and, in some cases, raising children, we poets are some-
times exactly expressive of the communities we belong
to, sometimes a little behind time, and many times ahead
of time with private visions given from sources we our-
selves are unable to explain.

The ten poets I have chosen to link in a tradition with
Sappho have been picked carefully. Emily Dickinson,
Amy Lowell, H.D., and Gertrude Stein are historic fore-
mothers of today's Lesbian poets. The six contemporary
women: Adrienne Rich, Audre Lorde, Pat Parker, Olga
Broumas, Paula Gunn Allen, and myself were chosen
after I was very positively influenced by an article in The
Hudson Review by Professor Mary J. Carruthers of the Uni-
versity of Illinois at Chicago. Carruthers titled her essay
"The Re-Vision of the Muse: Adrienne Rich, Audre Lorde,
Judy Grahn and Olga Broumas." She selected these par-
ticular people because "these four poets have voices that
are bold, even arrogant, in their common, urgent desire
to seize the language and forge with it an instrument for
articulating women. Not all women writing today write
this kind of poetry, not all poets who are Lesbians are
Lesbian poets, nor are all Lesbian poets always Lesbian."
She goes on to state that the "naming and defining" of the
word "Lesbian" is a central preoccupation of our work.[2]

We are using the word and the nature of "Lesbian," of
our special position as Lesbians, as a lens through which
to examine the rest of our society. "The word Lesbian
presents in paradigm the large issues of value in language,
of women's psyche and of social transformation, of alien-
ation and apocalypse, which these poets address" (294).

Even our position as outcast, a position well-articulated
in our work, helps to give us the special eyes through

which we see. Carruthers says, "*Lesbian* is also the essential outsider, woman alone and integral, who is oppressed and despised by traditional society, yet thereby free to use her position to re-form and re-member. She is a figure both of the satirist and the seer, a woman of integrity and power who is by nature and choice at odds with the world. *Lesbian* is also erotic connection, the primary energy of the senses which is both physical and intellectual, connecting women, a woman with herself, and women through time. Finally, *Lesbian* signifies a change of relationships, radical internal transformation; it is a myth of psychic rebirth, social redemption, and apocalypse" (294–5). We seek, she says, nothing less than the total transformation of our society.

From these interesting definitions, I drew some criteria of my own with which to formulate the ideas I have set forth in *The Highest Apple*. The contemporary poets whose work I have chosen to discuss include all four of the ones included in Mary Carruthers's analysis, plus the inimitable Pat Parker with her direct critique of American society from a Black as well as a feminist perspective, and Paula Gunn Allen, whose Laguna Pueblo voice adds critical dimension to the picture of Lesbian presence on this American continent. In addition to knowing the contemporary poets, I also lived with Paula for five years, and we were lovers at the time I wrote the first edition of *The Highest Apple*.

All of our work connects political, personal, sexual, historic, and mythic themes. We are only a few of the scores of Lesbian poets specializing in various aspects of what we are all doing together. Lesbian poetry, as you will see, is witty, detailed, personal, sexy, mythic, biting, eloquent, aesthetic, and profound, as our Lady Sappho was all these qualities also.

These essays make no attempt to provide a comprehensive overview of all the Lesbian poetry currently available in America. There are dozens of contemporary poets writing on Lesbian living, and Lesbians writing on contemporary living. Nor is this particular analysis attempting to specify "major" poets, nor in any way suggest that we current writers are to be compared with Sappho for her vitality. She is twenty-six centuries ahead of all of us, and is like a god to me. I am simply doing a comparison of ideas and themes as a way of beginning the outline for a Lesbian tradition of poetry. I selected the included voices on the basis of the fullness of their bodies of work, and of their development of certain ideas I wanted to pursue and compare. The primary story I am telling is of the re-emergence of the public Lesbian voice.

There is a tremendous need for some ambitious souls to undertake comprehensive and historical overviews of Lesbian content in women's poetry. There is a need for careful analysis and treatment of the work of such openly Lesbian poets as: Elsa Gidlow, who has published overtly Lesbian love poems since the 1920s, Chrystos, Marilyn Hacker, Susan Griffin, Minnie Bruce Pratt, Cherríe Moraga, Joy Harjo, June Jordan, Avotcja, Chocolate Waters, Cheryl Clarke, Irena Klepfisz, Jan Clausen, Donna Allegra, Willyce Kim, and dozens of others.

Poetry was important to the women's movement and especially so to Lesbians. More than one Lesbian has been kept from floundering on the rocks of alienation from her own culture, her own center, by having access, at least, to Lesbian poetry. We owe a great deal to poetry—two of our most important names, for instance: Lesbian and Sapphic. When has a larger group of humans, more pervasive behavior, and much more than this, the tradition of women's secret powers that such names imply, ever been named for a single poet? Through the centuries, our poetry has held that position in the branches of its lines, in fragments, and in the code of imagery. It is time, now, to begin to reveal that tradition.

I:
A HEART-SHAPED JOURNEY
TO A SIMILAR PLACE

And Sappho wrote this:

As the sweet-apple reddens on the bough-top, on the top of the topmost bough; the apple gatherers have forgotten it—no, they have not forgotten it entirely, but they could not reach it.[1]

I want to tell you a story, a story that particularly underlies much of the writing of the Lesbians of our era, as well as that of those feminists who accept the evidence of ancient (as well as modern) gynarchic societies. This is a story that says once upon a time, the world was very different from ours in quite specific and woman-related ways; in the world before and leading up to the poet Sappho there was a very considerable time, millennia, during which people were communal and spiritual and their culture was based primarily in womanly powers. Elizabeth Gould Davis gave us this information in *The First Sex* and Jane Ellen Harrison gave some confirmation of it in her ponderous studies of Greek mythic history, as have Marija Gimbutas with her archeology of ancient European gods, Evelyn Reed with her Marxian view, and Mary Daly with her philosophical unravelings of women's place in the universe. From Zora Neale Hurston and Margaret Murray we have gotten information of Black and white folk customs, many of which stem from pagan religions that went underground not so long ago as we might think. Robert Graves and some of the Jungian writers have long sought to give the Great Goddess her rightful position in the Western mind. Charlene Spretnak, Starhawk, Z. Budapest, Luisah Teish, and other women involved in what is generally called the "women's spirituality movement," along with modern American Indian–descended women such as Paula Gunn Allen and Joy Harjo and others writing about Indigenous women's traditions, like Canadian novelist Anne Cameron, have added to our understanding. All are surfacing with thousands of particles of fact and impression, picture and intuition, tradition and story, to give us our understanding of the world as a long, long story, of which the four- or five-thousand-year rise and spread of the patriarchal form is only one aspect, one era that developed within a complex matrix of other possible ways of being.

Our teachers have told that in those times in the ancient Mediterranean cultures that gave rise to Sappho, there were very great poets. Many of them, perhaps most of them, were women. We have been told that the goddess of India, Sarasvati, is the goddess of language and is a poet; she rides on a peacock because, just as a peacock's tail contains many eyes, so she, as a poet, needs many eyes to see all around herself deciphering what is true, or truly there for her perceiving. We know that the West African goddess Afrikete was goddess of language and poetry, as well as being a transvestite and a warrior, and that she preceded the trickster god Eshu, who took over many of her former functions.[2] We know it is said of Arabia that before the rise of patriarchal systems, this was a woman-centered culture, and that the seven most wondrous poets of the ancient world were women, Arab women, and every word of their work was destroyed when the newly forming patriarchal elements found it too competitive with their own worldview.

The island of Lesbos has a long woman-centered history, one more specifically remembered than some others, at least among Western peoples. Sappho's own home city of Mitylene was founded by Amazons who came from North Africa. After fighting their way across the Arabian Peninsula and Syria and establishing a shrine to Artemis at the city of Ephesos, they came across to the island of Lesbos where their leader, Myrina, established a special seaport city in honor of her sister, Mitylene. Some six hundred years later, Sappho was born there. Described as being of small stature with a dark complexion, the earliest coin representation shows a sharp-nosed woman who resembles the frizzy-haired women of Crete as they portrayed themselves on the wall friezes. Sappho had a daughter, Cleis, who she praised in her poetry and called "golden."

With these understandings I comprehend Sappho not as the "first woman poet," but as one of the last of that great era, and the only one to have some fragments survive. It is with this millennia-long story in mind that I understand both Homer and Sappho were drawing from and writing out of: a vast, rich, ancient, and woman-developed tradition that they shared in common. A common pool of stories, phrases, metaphors, and philosophical understandings had existed from time immemorial—in the same sense that Goddess-centered Gaelic myth, folk stories, and a wealth of language have existed and constitute a vast molten pool of wonderment from which modern bards such as W.B. Yeats, Dylan Thomas, or James Joyce drew their gold. How much greater must the accumulation have been, how much more intact, to have produced a Sappho. How many others must also have been produced whose work did not survive at all.

Sappho wrote to us from an island, a lavender-flowered island as travelers describe it, one of several that were cultural centers for her Greek world of 600 BCE. Like Rhodes, Crete, or Samos, Lesbos is an actual island. But to those of us holding Sappho in our mind's eye as *the* historic example both of Lesbianism and of Lesbian poetry, everything she represents lives on an island. That poetic island is separate from, even though it is central to, all of that ancient, ritualized, and mundane life of thriving, gorgeous Greece.

Sappho wrote from an island, an island of obvious natural beauty, grace, and apparent safety for women; she speaks of gentle gods and prays to a passionate, helpful Aphrodite. The love bonds established between herself and other women were open, accepted, acknowledged, of obvious social value and esteem. Her phrases concerning the loving of women are bordered by descriptions of rites and appropriate behavior to attract the positive attention of the gods.

In her world, Greek women in general were cloistered in extended family units. Yet they were central to themselves; they had to have been for her to write as she did. She lived on an island of women, in a company of women, from which she addressed all creation. And oh, how they listened.

What was her world like? Well, for one thing, it loved her. She was as popular in her time and the centuries immediately following as the Beatles have been in ours. But Sappho's poetry was left to languish as the ancient world changed, and the papyrus manuscripts were later claimed to have been burned by the Greek Church during the Medieval Christian era. We have 650 lines of a possible 10,000 that she wrote, thanks largely to other authors quoting her. Coins were minted in her land with her portrait on them. What was her own world like? She left us this:

> Coming down from heaven (?), from the mountaintop, Hither to me from Crete to this holy temple, where is your delightful grove of apple-trees, and altars smoking with incense; therein cold water babbles through apple-branches, and the whole place is shadowed by roses, and from the shimmering leaves the sleep of enchantment comes down; therein too a meadow, where horses graze, blossoms with spring flowers, and the winds blow gently . . . ; there, Cyprus, take . . . and pour gracefully into golden cups nectar that is mingled with our festivities. (Greek Lyric, 57)

No words even remotely resembling these that depict such a world of grace, beauty, and feminine magic have been written since her time. I believed for a long time that Sappho's world sounds so idyllic because she must have been wealthy. Yet no Lesbian of wealth has written anything resembling Sappho's descriptions. In fact, The Well of Loneliness came to us from the arms of the English upper class, and it is outrightly ugly in its unhappiness.

And what was the nature of Sappho's wealth? She praised it often enough: love, beauty, grace, flowers, appropriate behavior to attract the gods, lovely clothing, intelligence, tenderness. Her poems are filled with the color purple, the color gold, the sun, flowers, especially the violet and the rose, and altars, deer, groves of trees, and the stories of the gods. Love, she said, is a tale-weaver. Wealthy? We own no kind of money that would buy us Sappho's wealth. But it is not as if she did not ever speak of sorrow, or separation:

> and honestly I wish I were dead. She was leaving me with many tears and she said much and this in particular: 'Oh what bad luck has been ours, Sappho; truly I leave you against my will.' I replied to her thus: 'Go and fare well end remember me, for you know how we cared for you. If not, why then I want to remind you . . . and the good times we had. You put on many wreaths of violets and roses and (crocuses?) together by my side, and round your tender neck you put many woven garlands made from flowers and . . . with much flowery perfume, fit for a queen, you anointed yourself . . . and on soft beds . . . you would satisfy your longing (for?) tender . . .
>
> There was neither . . . nor shrine . . . from which we were absent, no grove . . . nor dance . . . sound (117)

It is no perfect, idyllic, trouble-free fantasy world that Sappho describes, nor is it the more ancient, apparently peaceful Anatolian goddess-worshipping society unearthed at Catal Huyuk by James Mellaart, where no sign of war existed. The war at Troy marked the beginning of the end of the matriarchal era for Western civilization and had already become the wellspring of literature for

Sappho's generation. She compares Helen's love for Paris to her own love for a woman she has known. Already the rich forest of Anatolia had been stripped to make ships for war. Sappho found the beauty of women far lovelier than all the mechanics of conquest. *Some say a host of cavalry, others of the infantry, and others of ships, is the most beautiful thing on the black earth, but I say it is whatsoever one loves*, the poem begins, as a splendid affirmation of her own love for Anactoria, *who is not here; I would rather see her lovely walk, and the bright sparkle of her face than the Lydians' chariots and armed infantry* (67). Tyrants lived in Sappho's time, and she was exiled during her life.[3] Pittacus, the name of the ruler of Lesbos during her time, would come to be a word meaning "tyrant."

Nevertheless, plenty remained of womanly powers. According to one writer on the nature of Sappho's times: "The customs of the Aeolians permitted more social and domestic freedom than was common in Greece. Aeolian women were not confined to the harem like Ionians, or subjected to the rigorous discipline of the Spartans. While mixing freely with male society, they were highly educated, and accustomed to express their sentiments."[4] The contribution this made to world culture was enormous, as indicated by this description: "Nowhere in any age of Greek history, or in any part of Hellas, did the love of physical beauty, the sensibility to radiant scenes of nature, the consuming fervor of personal feeling, assume such grand proportions and receive so illustrious an expression as they did in Lesbos" (Robison, 24). And Sappho wrote not to a tiny group of priestesses, but to the world at large—twenty-six centuries of it—even though much of her writing concerned something so personal, intimate, and, in ensuing centuries, so hidden as the love of women for each other.

What Was Sappho's Island Like?

What was Sappho's island like compared to our modern world? We can certainly tell something from examining the fragments of her work and then doing even a cursory comparison with a contemporary book of poetry by Lesbians. *Lesbian Poetry*, edited by Elly Bulkin and Joan Larkin, is a book containing most of the major themes articulated by the highly politicized, self-conscious movement of Lesbian feminism as it has developed in the United States since 1969, when its first voices were raised in overt, concerted number.[5]

From this comparison, we can tell something of what Sappho's life and times were like by looking in mirror perspective, at what they were not like. She did not write of Lesbian love out of a negative comparison with heterosexual love, nor by contrasting its merits with anything else, nor by rationalizations such as the following:

> *Men are bad, have mistreated women, sexually molested girls, abandoned and robbed us and therefore the bond between women is a desirable one—and we will be the height of tender, helpful rescuing of each other*

nor is Sappho's work bordered by circumstance:

> *Here we are consigned together in this boarding school, jail, convent, military barracks, where it has been made as difficult as possible for us to become lovers* nor is it bordered by walls of fear:

> I would love you gladly if I didn't know we would be punished for it; or I love you in spite of the punishment we go through for it . . . and here are some of the terrible murderous things that happen to Lesbians in our society, and indeed to all kinds of people in our society

nor is it bordered by any sense of restriction:

> I would love you but here I am locked in this castle, family, room, economic strait, social and moral judgment. Or, I do love you and how can I get us out of here—or, here we are, loving each other and trying to get each other out of here

There is a great deal of lamentation in the work of modern Lesbians, lamentation that Sappho did not speak of in what we know of her work. Indeed, she specified:

> For it is not right that there should be lamentation in the house of those who serve the Muses. That would not be fitting for us. (Greek Lyric, 161)

No Lesbian writer that I know of since Sappho (and I'm speaking particularly of Western literature) has written from a context that does not include some form of these strictures and suppressions. Most have hidden their Lesbianism altogether to prevent their work from being destroyed or completely neglected. Emily Dickinson's manuscripts came within a hair's breadth of destruction because she allowed so much Lesbian content to stay in them. Sappho's work indicated none of the restrictions, lack of safety, or fear of reprisal by husband, police, or

49

other patriarchal institution. The world her work created was not patriarchal.

After the earlier, cascading, patriarchal change recorded in Homer's account of the war at Troy, the change from a feminine-centered to a masculine-centered public world deepened. Sappho's world and the communal bonding that had sustained it nearly disappeared. The new world was masculine in its orientation and became gradually much more materially centered. Her gods were replaced by one god, and then by no god. Her work was destroyed except for fragments quoted in the work of male writers acknowledging her tremendous influence on them. A bit more (and the only complete poem) was found only recently at the turn of the century, on papyrus wrapped around a body from ancient Egypt. During the intervening centuries, the island of women as a central mind in a culture sank like Atlantis and went out of history.

Or not quite out of history. For I take the apple that Sappho said reddened on the topmost branch and was overlooked by the pickers—no, not so much overlooked as that they could not reach it—I take that apple to mean "feminine powers." I take it to mean the centrality of women to themselves, to each other and to their society. That apple remained, intact, safe from colonization and suppression, on the topmost branch, and in the fragmented history of a Lesbian poet and her underground descendants.

Poetry repeats and recreates the ceremonial myths which give human lives their meaning beyond the simple worm-like functions, eat, shit, move, reproduce, die, make good soil. Given a ceremonial story, we connect to a group; we connect to a time; we connect to a universe that has a place for us. *We mean*, and our meanings activate us. In the absence of such stories, we not only fall out of public life, we fall out of history, and out of the apple tree. We also fall out of mythic time, out of recognized, central social value. We fall out of poetry except as the objects of it, and as the underlying developers of it, "Muses." Without our names and stories of who we are, we fall out of meaning into a kind of no-world, a no-place of worms without even a worm's grace.

What the burning of Sappho's work, and the work of all the ancient women, and indeed more recently the burning of a large number of European women themselves, what all this destruction meant is that women in the West fell out of our own story. We fell, as Lucifer and Diana and paganism and the Fairy people and the whole Old Religion of Europe fell, and then we went to sleep. We fell into a sleep in the middle of our own story. The island that had sustained the core of our knowledge all but sank. Miraculously, the Island of Lesbos was sustained in little fragments; of the Lesbian Poet, barely nine hundred scattered phrases and lines from what had been more than nine volumes of 10,000 lines survived, but these were enough to form the memory of a tradition.

This tradition could be called the musings from a House of Women,[6] a women's tradition that must once have been highly developed. This central house, or island of feminine thought, was not isolated from its society, not underground or veiled. Rather it influenced the world at large, was called upon to do so as is a college or the Supreme Court or any modern institution of intelligence, artfulness, and responsibility.

Sappho, addressing another woman, precisely describes what happens when women are disconnected from the house of their Muses. In this poem the house of the Muses is called "Pieria," which is the name of their birthplace in Macedonia. The fruits of this house—art, intelligence, science, music, mathematics, poetry, story—she calls the "roses of Pieria." Women disconnected from this house will be lost to memory, Sappho says: truly a fate worse than mere personal death. It is cultural and spiritual death. Nor, she adds, will such disinherited women return from death in spirit-form,

> But when you die you will lie there, and afterwards there will never be any recollection of you or any longing for you since you have no share in the roses of Pieria; unseen in the house of Hades also, flown from our midst, you will go to and fro among the shadowy corpses. (Greek Lyric, 99)

From an Island to a Cloister

After the fall from public power of the women's house, the very names it must have had in the older societies were forbidden and forgotten, and the possibility of the essential bond between women, of Lesbian love, became a taboo subject. In the interest of forcing the total break with the homosexual, woman-centered, multi-godded, pagan past, literacy itself was forbidden for centuries to all women and most men.

The world of Western women as a community with a center, a public mind, a house of our own, became incorporated over the centuries gradually into the institution of the Christian Church, and then cloistered. Sporadic unions of women, the bonding of women in love and in the sharing of intellect, were formed, broken apart and reformed, were split apart and outlawed within the church. Around 1,200 AD, women in parts of Europe were thrown very thoroughly out of their power, which had been considerable, within the hierarchy of the church. Before the purge disallowing them to administer sacraments, there were nearly as many women abbots in Europe as there were men abbots. A medieval poem has remained, written from "one religious woman to another," according to John Boswell in his book *Christianity, Social Tolerance, and Homosexuality*. It is a lament to lost, almost eternally lost, love. The name of the writer, A., is unknown.

To G., her singular rose
From A.—the bonds of precious love.
What is my strength, that I should bear it,
That I should have patience in your absence?
Is my strength the strength of stones,
That I should await your return?
I, who grieve ceaselessly day and night
Like someone who has lost a hand or a foot?
Everything pleasant and delightful
Without you seems like mud underfoot.
I shed tears as I used to smile,
And my heart is never glad.
When I recall the kisses you gave me
And how with tender words you caressed my little breasts,
I want to die
Because I cannot see you . . .
For no one has been born into the world
So lovely and full of grace,

Or who so honestly
And with such deep affection loves me.
I shall therefore not cease to grieve
Until I deserve to see you again.
Well has a wise man said that it is a great sorrow
For a man to be without that
Without which he cannot live.
As long as the world stands
You shall never be removed from the core of my being.
What more can I say?
Come home, sweet love!
Prolong your trip no longer;
Know that I can bear your absence no longer.
Farewell.
Remember me.[7]

For centuries we have been without the independent institutions, the Islands of Lesbos, the Houses of the Muses and whatever their equivalents are in different ages and cultures—the midwife and market women guilds, the priestess schools, the art-letters-and-science colleges of women, the divinatory and healing societies, all the variety of forms the center of female will and intelligence has structured itself into in order to influence, guide, and lead society. Possessing such places, and such centrality to the people of their societies as Sappho had on Lesbos, is exactly what enables women to freely choose who they will or will not bond with. In their absence, Lesbianism has had at best a marginal, flimsy existence. And the apple of public, collective feminine power has hung on a secret tree, waiting.

In the absence of a Women's House or Island of free gathering, women became split from each other, from their mothers and sisters, and from themselves; the sexual bond between women went underground, became lamented, longed for. Besides the cloister, which has been for most centuries a strictly regulated, anti-Lesbian place, the other institution where women were gathered into one place was known as the harem in some cultures, the brothel and whorehouse in others. There, in groups where they are kept with their powers contained as symbols and toys of love for men, the women have bonded. But it is a sad love; it is the love women have for each other when they are in jail. The following poem is from China, written in the nineteenth century by one courtesan addressing another, and, like many other examples of modern poetry written by Lesbians addressing the women they love, the courtesan poem is a "rescue" fantasy.

Since the brothel has replaced the sacred grove, the island of the centrality of women has become a confinement. In the poem one of the lovers sings a sad song, a song of the memory of "another place," south of the river—and her lover longs to be able to take her away, to escape with her—to some place, a place that has no name since it has no existence, or rather, it has no existence because it has no name.

> For the Courtesan Ch'ing Lin
> To the tune "The Love of the Immortals"
> by Wu Tsao
>
> On your slender body
> Your jade and coral girdle ornaments chime
> Like those of a celestial companion
> Come from the Green Jade City of Heaven.

One smile from you when we meet,
And I become speechless and forget every word.
For too long you have gathered flowers,
And leaned against the bamboos,
Your green sleeves growing cold,
In your deserted valley:
I can visualize you all alone,
A girl harboring her cryptic thoughts.

You glow like a perfumed lamp
In the gathering shadows.
We play wine games
And recite each other's poems.
Then you sing "Remembering South of the River"
With its heart breaking verses. Then
We paint each other's beautiful eyebrows.
I want to possess you completely—
Your jade body
And your promised heart.
It is Spring.
Vast mists cover the Five Lakes.
My dear, let me buy a red painted boat
And carry you away.[8]

In the last couple of centuries, a new institution where girls and women are sometimes gathered together into one place has developed. It is the boarding school, where they have no autonomy, although they do at times have each other's attention and company. But boarding school, where girls are taken raw from the countryside or from newly colonized areas, breaks them apart from each other and from the "home" culture still further. Themes developing from this institution sometimes include the Lesbian matron as a villainous, hurtful character who rejects and punishes her charges in her role as guardian of the values of the state. Where the themes are of love, the love becomes riddled with hopelessness and romantic pain. They suffer, and they mourn their love and their loss of it. A novel by Lesbian poet Paula Gunn Allen chronicles this loss in a contemporary scene involving girls in a boarding school in New Mexico, some of whose foremothers were American Indians. She has been detailing the bleak sterility of the school:

She remembered the two sisters who, for a brief time did not look half dead. Sister Mary Grace and Sister Claire . . . Sister Mary Grace and one of the other boarders were playing the piano. Sister Claire had rolled up the sleeves of her habit, pinned the long veil back, decorously, as they often did when they were going to scrub the floor, instead she began to dance. She grabbed one of the girls and began to whirl her around. Sister Mary Grace turned to watch. The tall, heavy girl and the tiny, delicate nun danced and laughed with delight. The girl playing the piano struck up another tune. A polka. The girl dancing with Sister Claire went spinning off to sprawl, laughing, on a chair next to Ephanie. They crowed with delight. Sister Claire danced up to Sister Mary Grace. She drew Sister Mary Grace to her feet. She pulled her out onto the floor. They began to dance, laughing, giggling, like girls. Their faces growing rosy and gleaming from sweat and exertion. They danced the polka and laughed.

About a week later, Sister Claire was gone. Sent to another school. Or back to the mother house, the place where they were trained and where they lived when they retired. The girls talked about it in whispers. They eyed Sister Mary Grace. Whose face was heavy and dull with grief. Or with something that was not joy. They knew, sort of, what had happened. They were subdued. All of them. No one laughed or danced much the rest of the year. Sister Claire had been sent away and Sister Mary Grace must have wept.

The girls said, they must have been in love. And nodded to each other. And whispered. No one said anything about it being wrong. Ephanie thought now, all these years later, how glad they had all been that someone there was able to love. To laugh and shine and work and play and dance. And how very bereft they all felt when that love was sent away.[9]

From the island in the center of the mind of the Ancient World, the bond between women had retreated, first to the cloister and harem, then to the boarding school and prison, and ultimately to the spinster's spare bedroom by Emily Dickinson's time in the second half of the nineteenth century.

> *The moon has set and the Pleiades,* Sappho wrote, *it is midnight, and time goes by, and I lie alone* (Greek Lyric, 173).

But Sappho never lay so alone as Emily Dickinson lay with her solitary heart in her solitary bed in her solitary room in Amherst, Massachusetts, at the end of the Victorian age.[10] Child of a strict Calvinist father who discouraged her poetic thinking, and of a mother who apparently neglected to pay attention to her, Emily fell in love with women she could never go and live with, could not gather in a cloister with, was not closed in a boarding school with, could not openly hold close to her in her narrow and embarrassed bed. She could and did visit her beloved sister-in-law Sue across a meadow from her father's house. She poured out her love in poems and gave them to Sue. But Emily's room became her island of women, where she carried on a one-woman dialogue with the lovers she could not actually and formally and publicly gather into her life, and carried on a rousing, introspective one-woman dialogue with death and with the Calvinist god. She said of her room, "Here's freedom."

Adrienne Rich defined Dickinson as a great psychologist in her essay "Vesuvius at Home: The Power of Emily Dickinson," saying:

> Dickinson is *the* American poet whose work consisted in exploring states of psychic extremity. For a long time, as we have seen, this fact was obscured by the kinds of selections made from her work by timid if well-meaning editors. In fact, Dickinson was a great psychologist, and like every great psychologist, she began with the material she had at hand: herself. She had to possess the courage to enter, through language, states which most people deny or veil with silence.[11]

The basis of Dickinson's extreme isolation was economic as well as social; her father kept her at home as his companion, saw no reason to give her a single penny, and allowed her no traveling even to see a doctor. This situation was typical for white women of the middle classes in the nineteenth century. Several of her physical needs were taken care of, but she was always on a leash. Her mind was not recognized, and neither was the autonomy of her body.

From the content of her letters it is clear that she loved the woman who lived in the house adjoining her father's, her sister-in-law, Susan Gilbert Dickinson. This love and these letters contained expressions of a physical passion that went far beyond even the highly romantic content of correspondence between women in that day. Apparently, at one time, this love was reciprocated. "Susie, will you indeed come home next Saturday, and be my own again, and kiss me as you used to?" The erotic content of Emily's letters to Susan Dickinson was cut from earlier publications and has been re-membered by Lillian Faderman in *Surpassing the Love of Men*.[12] Emily loved Sue—who withdrew from her sexually though not emotionally—all her life.

According to biographer Rebecca Patterson in *The Riddle of Emily Dickinson*,[13] a second woman Emily fell in love with when she was twenty-eight was Kate Scott, who probably made an amorous offer that Emily was in no position to accept. Highly adventurous and lively, Kate managed to travel by marrying husbands who required her nursing skills and companionship, visiting health spas located in Europe. After seeing two of them into the grave, she inherited money that was hers alone, years after being attracted to, and losing, Emily.

The first thing that Kate, who nicknamed herself "Tommy" and, even more dykishly, "Thomas," did with her middle-aged financial independence was to take a female lover, a young woman to whom she was companion and teacher. A surviving diary reveals the highly personal information that Kate gave the young woman a gold ring as token of her love, and that they nicknamed each other Mr. and Mrs. Pump. They considered themselves married, in other words. Kate was the "Mr." to her woman lover (Patterson, 129). All this happened years after Kate Scott went to Amherst and wooed the young Dickinson for a two-year period, then apparently decided the love was hopeless and broke it off (an event Emily seems to have taken as a major theme of heartbreak, of desire and loss, in her work). The summer after Kate's letter rejecting any hope of their continuing and impossible love, Emily wrote of two women who had married one summer:

Ourselves were wed one summer—dear—
Your Vision—was in June—
And when Your little Lifetime failed,
I wearied—too—of mine—

And overtaken in the Dark—
Where You had put me down—
By Some one carrying a Light—
I—too—received the Sign.

'Tis true—Our Futures different lay—
Your Cottage—faced the sun—
While Oceans—and the North did play—
On every side of mine
'Tis true, Your Garden led the Bloom,
For mine—in Frosts—was sown—

And yet, one Summer, we were Queens—
But You—were crowned in June—[14]

Dickinson, lacking a common language with which to describe her love for other women and her own dykely qualities, made up one of her own in her poetry. Two women together were "queens." She spoke of herself as an "earl" and as having had a "boyhood." How did Kate want her to be, she wrote during the height of their passion in the late 1850s; did Kate want her to be a queen or a page? Tall or short? She, Emily, would be anything, as long as it suited Kate. But the match did not suit Kate. She did not choose to stay in Amherst—and how could she have, where would she have lived? Nor did she persuade Emily to come away with her. How could she have? Where would they have gone with no money? They would not have survived a week. Yet, they played hopeful come here-go away with each other for as long as two years.

Split from the women she loved, Dickinson was split away from herself, a state of mental division she acted out by refusing to sit in the same room with visitors when they came to see her. Dressed perpetually in white like the ghost she may have thought of herself as being, Dickinson sat in a separate room and spoke to her guests through a half-closed door. Her rage is really evident in this eccentricity. If she could not come into the room as who she was and who she wanted to be, well then, she wouldn't come into it at all. The love she had wanted, and which represented appreciation, intellectual companionship, a whole world blooming before her, that love had come and offered itself to her when she was without the means and the social support to accept; it had been given to her "without the Suit, Riches and Name and Realm," as she wrote in 1874:

Frigid and sweet Her parting Face—
Frigid and fleet my Feet—
Alien and vain whatever Clime
Acrid whatever Fate.

Given to me without the Suit
Riches and Name and Realm—
Who was She to withhold from me
Hemisphere and Home?[15]

"Hemisphere and home" could not be hers in this life. From the island of her woman's mind and isolation, Dickinson wrote repeatedly of death as a possibly happy place, a place where she could be reunited with her love, and with herself, a place where she could find her name:

The Things that Death will buy
        Are Room—
Escape from Circumstances—
And a Name—[16]

For Dickinson, writing from inside the island of her head, death constituted her only hope that herself and her "flower," by which I believe she meant her sexual, intelligent, worldly, womanly being, could be reunited. Death was the place where reunion with her own womanly powers and love could take place:

Here, where the Daisies fit my Head
'Tis easiest to lie
And every Grass that plays outside
Is sorry, some, for me.

Where I am not afraid to go
I may confide my Flower—
Who was not Enemy of Me
Will gentle be, to Her.

Nor separate, Herself and Me
By Distances become—
A single Bloom we constitute
Departed, or at Home—

(475)

She spoke for nearly all white women of the Victorian age, since she simply represented a more extreme form of many of their lives, which were in every way restricted. Dickinson articulated some of the most extreme fragmentation Lesbian poets have undergone.

Lacking a language to speak for the special passion she felt and could not satisfy, she created an internal panorama of the mind and the emotions, of our connections to the elemental ways of being and perceiving; lacking a language specific to her own life, she created one that would be of fascination and use to her society for generations to come.

Coming Out of the Cloister with a Cigar

From the room alone, from the isolate, structured life of the nineteenth century, Lesbians and Lesbian poetry turned a corner, coming out of the Victorian age with ci-gar-smoking Amy Lowell for a leader. Her upper-class literary family indulged her as the youngest child, allowed her tomboy childhood, supported her poetry, and accepted her eccentric dyke adulthood. Her longtime marriage to actress Ada Dwyer Russell (nicknamed "Peter") and her own robust dykeliness were public knowledge. Much of her poetry was overtly Lesbian, and perhaps more importantly, she saw the world, even the powerful sun, as a woman and herself as its lover:

The Wheel of the Sun

I beg you
Hide your face from me.
Draw the tissue of your head-gear
Over your eyes.
For I am blinded by your beauty,
And my heart is strained,
And aches,
Before you.

In the street,
You spread a brightness where you walk,
And I see your lifting silks
And rejoice:
But I cannot look up to your face.
You melt my strength,
And set my knees to trembling.
Shadow yourself that I may love you,
For now it is too great a pain.[17]

Many of her lines of love to the world as female are
overtly Lesbian, as in:

And this paper is dull, crisp, smooth
virgin of loneliness
Beneath my hand.

(210)

Given the special role the hand plays in Lesbian love-
making, this passage is especially erotic—for Lesbians.
She felt protective in her role as a lover, saying in "A
Shower,"

How I love it!
And the touch of you upon my arm
As you press against me that my umbrella
May cover you.

(213)

Lowell's poetry, and most especially her love poetry,
does not take place in a cloister or a tiny room in one cor-
ner of her father's house. Her settings are most often a
garden or the countryside. The garden is still a protected
place, but at least it is outdoors, in the open, and best of all
the woman beloved is present in the flesh, walking beside
her, loving her. Nowhere in Lowell's work is the beloved a
rejecting lost heartbreaker, longed for in later life, as the
beloved women are in some of Dickinson's lines. The poems
to Ada and to the womanly world are not the memory of
lost love, not the longing of unrequited and helpless ado-
lescence, not the desire and longing for escape together
from an unbearable life. Though Lowell does perceive the

city as a threatening place in "The Taxi," it is still in the context of love as a haven:

> Streets coming fast,
> One after the other,
> Wedge you away from me,
> And the lamps of the city prick my eyes
> So that I can no longer see your face.
> Why should I leave you,
> To wound myself on the sharp edges of the night?[18]

However, most of her love poems are not this urban; they use imagery of flowers, of which she knew a great deal, having been born into an estate that was rich with landscape and having a lifetime love of gardening. "Ah, Dear, I love you," she simply ends one poetic description of two lovers who are flowers, one purple, one crimson ("Frimaire," *Complete Poetical Works*, 219). In "Reflections," she sees in the beloved's eyes much more than a garden, she sees a whole world of grace and beauty, and a woman's hand reaching in to grasp it:

> When I looked into your eyes
> I saw a garden
> With peonies, and tinkling pagodas
> And round-arched bridges
> Over still lakes.
> A woman sat beside the water
> In a rain-blue, silken garment.
> She reached through the water
> To pluck the crimson peonies
> Beneath the surface,

But as she grasped the stems,
They jarred and broke into white-green ripples;
And as she drew out her hand,
The water-drops dripping from it
Stained her rain-blue dress like tears.

(208)

But that world does not exist, and the image breaks, and the poem ends with wistful sorrow. Lowell's work was heavily criticized for its Lesbian content during the 1920s, and there is no hint of her Lesbianism in the work chosen for anthologizing. Had she not smoked a cigar and had the habit of sitting with her feet on the desk, I would not have spotted and recognized her as a dyke in my own isolated early days. Born the same year as Gertrude Stein, she died much earlier, living in fear, apparently, that she would outlive her lover Ada Russell. She died in 1923 at the age of forty-nine, having set the stage through her work with the Imagist movement for her contemporary, H.D., who was just launching her own work in 1923, as also was Lowell's other natural contemporary, Gertrude Stein.

As Lowell did for Ada Russell, Stein made certain her lifetime female lover is present in her work. In her photographs as well as in the texts of her writing, Alice B. Toklas is included. She is present as the lover, even publicly so, tucked inside Stein's carefully coded verbal disguises.

For all of the tremendous range of her mind, Stein's settings rarely leave the interior of a house, usually taking place in one room; mundane objects of a room are given the same value in her sentences as persons, and indeed so are the verbs, adjectives, articles, and conjunctions. Exiles from a still brawling, anti-intellectual Western America,

Stein and Toklas created their own little island in Paris, with a coterie of Lesbian and also Gay friends, and with a peculiarly French form of cloister: the literary and artistic salon. The two Jewish women brought into their self-defined salon world every artist and writer of any importance within their sphere of influence, all men. But though she drew stimulation from men, sat among them in her house, taught them and influenced them, Stein's work centered almost entirely on women, and—basic to this—on solving the problems of expressing and naming a Lesbian life in a world that forbade doing so.

Her first novel, Q.E.D. (abbreviation for the Latin phrase meaning "things as they are") is about three young Lesbians involved in a love triangle. The solution of the triangle situation is the book's focal point, rather than the subject of Lesbianism and its relation to the external world. The Lesbianism, in fact, is so taken for granted in the text that she achieved what has been a goal for Lesbian prose writers who have succeeded her: writing a Lesbian novel in which the characters just "happen" to be Lesbian. Small wonder that in an era that saw The Well of Loneliness[19] become widely known with its wringing plea for "acceptance" for the terrible aberration, Stein's simple novel of three lovers was so unpublishable that she shelved it for the duration of her life. "Things as they are" was not a marketable commodity even among literary folk in her day (nor are they now). She believed that the book would reach publication within a decade or so of her death in 1946. But not until 1973 was it possible to get more than an underground photocopied version of Q.E.D. (I seem to recall having such a manuscript pass through my hands, in

1970 or 1971). After putting away as unpublishable such overt reference to the facts of her own life, Stein developed a style that could include this personal content without evoking the taboo.

Richard Kostelanetz says in his introduction to *The Yale Gertrude Stein*, a collection published in 1983, "In *Tender Buttons*, which was begun in 1911 and finished the following year, her aim was the creation of texts that described a thing without mentioning it by name."[20] She surrounded the subject without ever naming it. And in doing so, she found a solution to that central problem of her own forbidden existence—for how can a creative writer write without having the free use of her own life to do it with? In solving that huge problem, by surrounding the subject of Lesbianism and of her love and the rich, lively life she had with Alice Toklas without ever naming them, she did the same for all her ideas; she surrounded all of them with provocative verbal structures without ever naming them. In so doing she began to teach the entire English-speaking world some new tools with which to think—to think without using names.

Stein disseminated the essence of the forbidden—and untouchable—Lesbian apple into the homey atmosphere of her work in the most subtle of ways, most of which have barely been decoded in our era. Meanwhile, her contemporary H.D. was placing it, and the centrality of women's power, into some very external contexts. Like Stein, H.D. is a giant twentieth-century poet. (Amy Lowell is a door opener, by contrast, having died too soon to develop the huge body of work necessary for her to reach their stature.) H.D. developed the ancient metaphor of the orchard as a sacred place. She described the orchard not just as a secular garden with some wishful Venus statues, as Lowell did, but as a real grove of real women's power.

What has been best known of H.D.'s work is its thinnest, earliest parts featuring the spareness of clean imagery sought by a generation of American poets as they broke with the more lush descriptions of the nineteenth century. "Imagist" was the tag for what they were doing, and H.D. was considered the best. Yet, pretty as "whirl up, sea" is as an image, it is a puff of air compared to the full-bodied bulk of H.D.'s work as it grew to fruition in the context of her forty-year-long Lesbian marriage-allegiance to the woman Bryher, which began in 1919.

Raised a Moravian in Pennsylvania (born in Bethlehem), H.D. watched her first marriage, to Richard Aldington, deteriorate as the First World War gradually took his attention from her world of poetry and beauty to the mechanized destruction that consumed two generations of European, American, and Asian men. Pregnant, alone, devastated by despair, she was literally rescued by young Bryher, daughter of a shipping magnate. Bryher took her to the Greek Islands where she recovered, though she was to suffer several more breakdowns in her life. Her work, more specifically descended from Sappho's than that of the other Lesbian poets under discussion, centered on defining the essential womanly mythos for our time. She found the most substantial image in Helen, another great beauty who endured another Great War.[21] For H.D. the "apple," or "island," of women's centrality was not Lesbianism itself, but it was her Lesbian partnership that enabled her to see her society and the relation of Woman to it.

Islands were recurrent in her relationship with Bryher and to her own art; it was to an island Bryher took her to have her child, a daughter, Perdita. H.D.'s frame of reference was "island"—Greece, and then ancient Egypt, especially; in Helen she constructed an image of hiding out from the war on a special, white island. H.D. used classical mythology and Hermetic philosophy as a code of her own with which to lay down a philosophical exploration of female power in a masculine world. Bryher, too, used "island" to describe who she was; she named herself for an island off Scotland: Bryher. And the two of them together, even when sometimes involved triangularly with a man, constituted a little island of cultivation and protection for their literary work.

Although overtly Lesbian sexual imagery is more sparse in H.D.'s work than it is in Lowell's, near the end of her writing life she wrote these supreme erotic Lesbian lines:

you say there is dried fruit

in the amphora and the wine-jars,
but I would wander in the Elysian-fields
and find the Tree for myself—for myself—

with a special low down-sweeping burdened bough,
low enough so that I could kneel
and savor the fragrance of the cleft fruit

on the branch, intoxicant;
I would be intoxicated with the scent of fruit,
O, holy apple, O, ripe ecstasy[22]

The hot richness of that particular apple did not reach far enough to touch my young life, even though H.D. was writing those words in 1959, the year I went to live with my first lover. We knew nothing of Lesbian poets in the past—except Sappho—and as two lovers we constituted an "island" as well, one of extreme secrecy and isolation. Yet only ten years later, in 1969, I would write a set of poems that set an overtly Lesbian figure in a context of other women. "Carol in the park, chewing on straws" is one of seven portraits in *The Common Woman Poems*. In this poem, the woman is definitely out of the garden and out of her father's house; she is also free of coded language and covert messages. In the poem she is squarely located in a public park, not passing through, but staying there in the open, chewing on straws, contemplating her life. She has a woman lover with whom she lives, and the poem makes it clear that they keep this a secret from others by lying about it. The poem reveals the secret of their life together and sets them into a context with other "common" women, women who also have secrets and dire needs of one kind or another, that are also being made public. The Lesbian is set into a context of other women, regular, ordinary American women. She is "cloistered" only by virtue of the closet of secrecy that cuts her off from other people, and so her life is an unknown thing being revealed. She dreams:

> On weekends, she dreams of becoming a tree;
> a tree that dreams it is ground up
> and sent to the paper factory, where it
> lies helpless in sheets, until it dreams
> of becoming a paper airplane and rises
> on its own current; where it turns into a
> bird, a great coasting bird that dreams of becoming

more free, even, than that—a feather, finally, or
a piece of air with lightning in it.[23]

She is angry energy, and a thunderstorm. By 1971 Carol
in the park with her woman lover has been "decloistered"
altogether; she now lives, along with a poem titled "A His-
tory of Lesbianism," in a bold little blue book called *Edward
the Dyke and Other Poems*, a title chosen precisely for its
use of the magical underground taboo word. This was not
the first time the word "Lesbian" had appeared in poetry,
but probably no poetry book ever had "dyke" in it.

Though my voice was the first of the poets considered
in this particular lineage of lines and images to use and
publish overtly Gay terminology and experience[24]—"I am
the dyke in the matter / the other . . . I am the bulldyke
/ the bulldagger"—I was joined rapidly by Black activist
Pat Parker. Responding to Biblical Eve being created of
Adam's rib, Pat had already written: "I, woman, must be
/ the child of myself,"[25] and, in a poem dedicated to her
mother, "All of these / real people— / are real, / live in the/
flesh dykes" ("Cop-Out," 109). We worked as a team doing
readings for years. We heard Audre Lorde read her work
on the West Coast, and she had visited both of us, spend-
ing long hours especially talking to Pat. Soon, Lorde came
all the way out of the closet in her work and public image.
This must have been a particularly terror-ridden passage
given the threat that as Black Lesbians they could lose the
support of the Black community and be left to drift alone
in a racist and homophobic world. Lorde had already es-
tablished her poetic reputation, growing out of the beat-
nik roots of her development (with her early co-heart in
poetry, Diane DiPrima) into her own highly individual

mythic-lyric-political voice, within the context of the Black political and cultural movements of the 1960s. She had published First Cities and Cables to Rage by 1970.

Adrienne Rich had achieved recognition among mainstream poetic audiences as early as publication of her first book, A Change of Worlds, in 1953. She shifted voices as the feminist and Lesbian/feminist ideology and activism geared up in the early seventies, infusing her careful, socially analytical poetry with compelling feminism, an internal, close-in voice. She quickly drew the attention of a great many women with her 1973 volume, Diving into The Wreck. She then stepped firmly onto an overtly Lesbian poetic literary path with Twenty-One Love Poems, written between 1974 and 1976, and The Dream of a Common Language, published in 1978.

Olga Broumas surfaced with five Lesbian love poems, Caritas, in 1976, and Beginning with O in 1977, chosen for the Yale Series of Younger Poets. Earlier, in 1975, she had written "Twelve Aspects of God" in conjunction with twelve oil paintings by artist Sandra McKee, exhibited at a gallery in Eugene, Oregon. She took the stage as a Lesbian poet from the beginning of her public presentations of her art. The erotic/sacred content of her work, as well as her classical frame of reference (which, as a native of Greece, she is surely entitled to, if anyone is), places her directly in a line with Sappho.

Paula Gunn Allen is another poet who, like Lorde and Rich, had already fixed a place for herself in a different sphere, in her case the sphere of burgeoning American Indian poetry, literature, and criticism. Having participated in the Bay Area poetic community since the early sixties, as well as being heavily published in academic circles, she gained attention in the Lesbian feminist community dramatically in 1981, with her poem "Beloved Women" and the accompanying essay "Beloved Women: Lesbians in American Indian Cultures."[26] Her work was both startling and exciting in that it acknowledged for the first time a special office of Lesbianism held among some Native American tribes in former times.

The overlapping work of these six writers articulate the major themes and definitions of Lesbian poetry as it developed from 1969 into the 1980s.[27]

The first thing we did was find a new setting. Beyond the city park of Carol with her contemplative straws, the city itself became the new location for the poems of Lesbian poets, even while urban life is often seen as a hostile environment full of danger, masculine technology, violence, dirt, and opposition to the Lesbian bond. The new "island" of Lesbianism includes acceptance, even positive use of, the outcast state from which the new Lesbians will build a "Lesbian Nation." To be sure, we have not lost our gardens. My set of poems "Confrontations with the Devil in the Form of Love" is completely dependent on the presence of apple trees, though it is otherwise urban in reference. But in recent Lesbian poetry, the garden is no longer the major place; in fact it may have become a paltry, undersized container for larger ambitions. Audre Lorde describes going hand in hand with her lover into her backyard garden after a winter of difficulty in a poem called "Walking Our Boundaries":

The sun is watery warm
our voices
seem too loud for this small yard

too tentative for women
so in love
the siding has come loose in spots
our footsteps hold this place
together
as our place
our joint decisions make the possible
whole.[28]

She clearly states that the place itself is formed by their
Lesbian marriage, which has outgrown itself.

A Crossing to a Heart-Shaped Place

During this time, Lesbians are leaving cloistered, iso-
lated rooms and safely enclosed gardens to cross into public
life. It is during the period from 1973 to 1977 that some of
the poets write of a "crossing" in which a pair of Lesbians
make a perilous modern urban journey in which they
have an insight about their situation with respect to the
rest of the world. The most developed of these is my own
"A Woman Is Talking to Death," written in February of
1973 and published a year later.

This crossing takes place on the Bay Bridge, on which
the two Lesbians witness a motorcycle accident. A very
careless young white man standing in the middle of the
lane is killed in this accident, and the white policemen
and court system blame the death upon the Black driver.
The poem is a series of meditations on both modern ur-
ban and historical situations, especially centering on the
position of women, but with cross-reference to people of
color in American society, among many other things. The

poem confronts and challenges the Christian mythic system of celebrating the heroism of martyred white men by revealing it as arrogant, as wasteful, and as intolerably harmful to the people of the society who don't fit that definition. The poem's solution is that the women (and their "lovers") will not continue to be victimized by the myth of the hero, or male or white supremacy, of modern industrialization, or "death" as the antagonist is called in the poem. "Real loving" is that decision to no longer agree to victimization. In fact, when the poem ends, the women and those who can connect to them will go somewhere else, out of the myth; they will stop working for it, and go to be with each other and to prepare the way for a different world. And the myth of death shall be left behind, and shall be "poor."

In the poem, the drastic intercultural and intergender oppressions which are everywhere manifest and in which all of us are completely enmeshed, are offset only by a delicate refrain: "My lover's teeth are white geese / flying above me / my lover's muscles are rope ladders / under my hands." The image conjures a ship's sails and a ship's ladders, not a modern ship but an old- fashioned vessel, perhaps going to an ancient land. The two lovers together, now one flying above and now the other, constitute the ship. They are taking each other someplace. Geese, incidentally, is another word for Gay, as in the phrase "Gay as a goose."[29]

Olga Broumas has a crossing poem, published in 1977 in her first book, *Beginning with O*. Broumas's awakening of Sleeping Beauty, of the slumbering goddess within us waking to the memory of a woman's love on her lips, is set in the city, like most of Rich's "Twenty-One Love Poems" and all but the refrain of "A Woman Is Talking to Death."

City-center, mid-
traffic, I
wake to your public kiss. Your name
is Judith, your kiss a sign

to the shocked pedestrians, gathered
beneath the light that means
stop
in our culture
where red is a warning, and men
threaten each other with final violence: *I will drink*
your blood. Your kiss
is for them

a sign of betrayal, your red
lips suspect, unspeakable
liberties as
we cross the street, kissing
against the light, singing, *This*
is the woman I woke from sleep, the woman that woke
me sleeping.[30]

In a place that is located in the very center of the city, the Lesbians are kissing each other awake with a public kiss, are accepting an outcast status, are in fact holding each other and kissing against the light on purpose. Their outcast status is the new island from which they will view the rest of the world, and comment upon it; and at last the island of women—however uncomfortably—is located out of the tight little rooms, the half-sheltered gardens and the dreamlike orchards of the lover's mind. It does not have to be exotically, toleratedly perched in the rarified air of the upper class with Lowell, nor exiled in the safety of Switzerland with H.D. and Bryher; now the love is public, is out in the open in America. It is in the world. And as such it is a step in reclaiming the world, for women, and of renaming the stories of being out in the world, this time with women in them. The bridge to the island of ourselves has begun.

The first collection of works by women of color with many of the authors openly identified as Lesbian is titled *This Bridge Called My Back*. For these writers, their own minds and bodies and spirits constitute of necessity the bridge of flesh that crosses from one culture to another, from one worldview to another. They are making the crossing from race to race as well as locating a place to be women together. In so doing they hold out promise that all of us will be led to a much larger, fuller, more intricate "island" than anything we could ever imagine as one group alone. African American-Lesbian activist poet Pat Parker crossed all the way into celebrating her lesbian life, from a discouraging first attempt at lesbian sex that ends, "you shudder & take 2 aspirin," in 1970 to inspiriting lines of the mid-1980s:

> I have a lover
> who is strong—
> Does not jump when I holler
> Does not take all my words
> as edicts from God—
>
> I have a lover
> who is loving—
> holds me when I am tired

rubs me when I am tight with anger—
I have a lover
who understands
Does not think me crazy
when I share my dreams
Does not think me foolish
when I am the fool
("I have a lover", p. 411, The Complete Works of Pat Parker)

Just fifteen years of public lesbian organizing made that difference for her. However, the heart-shaped places of lesbian bonding across cultural and racial differences do not always land us in similar places. Parker said in a 1980 speech, speaking of "the revolution" as something that would include people of color, women, and Gay people, that it would not be "easy, or neat, or quick." That some crossings are difficult or impossible in helping women bond is clearly stated in her poem responding to an incident in a 1971 Lesbian activists' meeting in which a white woman made an invisibilizing racist comment:

> . . . have you ever tried to hide?
> in a group
> of women
> hide
>
> yourself
> slide between the floor boards
> slide yourself away child
> away from this room
> & your sister
> before she notices
> your Black self &

her white mind
        slide your eyes
            down
away from the other Blacks
     afraid—a meeting of eyes
& pain would travel between you
     change like milk to buttermilk
        a silent rage
          SISTER! your foot's smaller,
but it's still on my neck.
("Have you ever tried to hide?", p. 35, *The Complete Works of Pat Parker*)

The poem calls on oblivious white Lesbians to cultivate awareness of diversity and become sensitive to the harm of careless or outright racist speech.

Audre Lorde calls for us all to "stop killing / the other / in ourselves / the self that we hate / in others" ("Between Ourselves," *The Black Unicorn*, 112–14). The bridge to others is herself. The bridge to herself is the bridge to others. In Lorde's poem "October," she is her own bridge, and she calls on Seboulisa, mother of power, to help her with her crossing:

Spirits
of the abnormally born
live on in water
of the heroically dead
in the entrails of snake.
Now I span my days like a wild bridge
swaying in place
caught between poems like a vise

I am finishing my piece of this bargain
and how shall I return?

Seboulisa, mother of power
keeper of birds
fat and beautiful
give me the strength of your eyes
to remember
what I have learned
help me to attend with passion
these tasks at my hand for doing.
Carry my heart to some shore
that my feet will not shatter
do not let me pass away
before I have a name
for this tree
under which I am lying.
Do not let me die
still
needing to be stranger.[31]

The call is for a new island, some new shore that does
not shatter underfoot, a name—a name for a place that is
already happening, as the poet says she is already lying
under the tree of it.

Adrienne Rich's "Twenty-One Love Poems," written
in 1974 after she had read "A Woman Is Talking to Death,"
contains a crossing. This is a ferry crossing in which two
Lesbian lovers are confined in the cabin with the other
couples, straight people, newlyweds, representing the
most openly expressive form of the heterosexual culture
that has been so prohibitive of the homosexual culture.
And in the poem the narrator puts her hand on her lover's

knee, openly, and has never felt closer to her than at this moment when they can, at last, be public. They can be public because everyone is so seasick no one is going to notice that they are doing this taboo thing. In "Twenty-One Love Poems," Rich is calling for a love based in reality: "I told you from the first I wanted daily life, / this island of Manhattan is island enough for me."[32] She wants a Lesbian life that is not exotic, in other words, not in exile, not hidden and not located on a fantasy island, but rather is right there in the contemporary urban island of Manhattan, as a full and public life.

And yet, how to do this? For what is the meaning of it, the *ritual* significance? What is the story we can tell ourselves of our doings that gives our lives meaning? What connects us back to the Roses of the Muses, and to the highest apple that is ourselves? "No one has imagined us,"[33] Rich says. And therefore, we have no way of imagining ourselves; until we can, we have no real, meaningful being. In the last of the "Twenty-One Love Poems," she locates a new island. "Stonehenge," she says, but not really Stonehenge, rather it is something like Stonehenge, a place of the past that is actually waiting for us in the future. It is a special, measured place where she as a woman and as an open Lesbian has chosen to go, to "draw this circle," a circle in which she and her lovers can live, and can envision their lives into a meaningful scheme, a new dream.

What Is the Nature of This Dream, This New Island?

"Is my strength the strength of stones, / That I should await your return?" the medieval Lesbian named only "A.," as I said earlier, wrote seven hundred years ago (Bankier and Lashgari, 24–25).

Apparently the strength of stones is what is called for, at least as it appears in the imagery of the Lesbian poets of this discussion. In Lorde's words, in "Woman," the new stones are located in a place wherein the "commonest rock / is moonstone and ebony opal / giving milk to all my hungers" ("Woman," The Black Unicorn, 82). She makes clear who the "stones" will be in the "Journeystones I-IX," a set of portraits of women she knows. The stones are each woman and ourselves, and each other in ourselves, even in our apparent oppositions of race and class, of moonstone and ebony opal.

Olga Broumas describes three muses casting stones on an earthen platter, "till the salt veins aligned, and she read the cast":

Whatever is past
And has come to an end
cannot be brought back by sorrow
("Triple Muse," Beginning with O, 9)

For Paula Gunn Allen, as for the other Lesbian poets, the new island is a psychic as well as a material place, a shared vision, one especially keenly visualized during the sexual closeness with a lover. The new world to be envisioned is right here, in the everyday life we have in common with so many women and ultimately so many people. We will not transform what we perceive as a very limited, one-sided half-civilization. To use words from Rich:

this still unexcavated hole
called civilization, this act of translation, this half-world,
(Dream of a Common Language, 27)

cannot be transformed enough by violent revolution, and certainly not by transcendence *from* it, by escape or by constructing a "heaven" in the skies. Rather we will transform it by living in it, while yet holding a second vision, a new dream/vision, in our minds at the same time. In defining the precise dimensions of that dream, by attempting to live it, and by helping each other to see and feel and express it, we will affect the world, by changing its mind.[34]

"Beauty of the moon rests directly on the darkness of the sky," Paula Gunn Allen says. By repeatedly placing dark and light images side by side, she is positing a harmonious whole, a possible interdependence, rather than a set of unalterable oppositions. In "Moonstream," Paula describes the interplay of dark and light:

> We walked into the lodge of the moon
> and lay
> at the center of the stones
> that give us light
> you placed your hand deep in shadow hollows
> and the flowers deep in my mooncave
> spilled their perfume over you
> moon woman followed our ways—
> spilling her perfume between my legs
> knees rising in the shadows
> mountain peaks holding moon
> perfectly in shadow framed.[35]

Only a one-sided patriarchal mind could separate the brightness of the moon from the dark sky that holds it and makes it possible. The Lesbian at the heart of her mind knows that dark and light are the same thing. To quote H.D., "l'île blanche is l'île noire" (the white island is the black island). When we understand this, we can put our broken selves back together. We have already begun to uncover the stones necessary to build another island.

Adrienne Rich, in The Dream of a Common Language, locates a new island,

> Not Stonehenge
> simply nor any place but the mind
> casting back to where her solitude,
> shared, could be chosen without loneliness,
> not easily nor without pains to stake out
> the circle, the heavy shadows, the great light.
> I choose to be a figure of that light,
> half-blotted by darkness, something moving
> across that space, the color of stone
> greeting the moon, yet more than stone:
> a woman. I choose to walk here. And to draw this circle.[36]

And she goes on from this to "Transcendental Etude," a poem in which she finds her way to a new rock, a new sense of home and of homesickness:

> Such a composition has nothing to do with eternity,
> the striving for greatness, brilliance—
> only with the musing of a mind
> one with her body, experienced fingers quietly pushing
> dark against bright, silk against roughness,
> pulling the tenets of a life together
> with no mere will to mastery,
> only care for the many-lived, unending

forms in which she finds herself, becoming now
                    the shard of broken glass
slicing light in a corner, dangerous
to flesh, now the plentiful, soft leaf
that wrapped round the throbbing finger,
                    soothes the wound;
and now the stone foundation, rockshelf further
forming underneath everything that grows.
                    (77)

The idea of the woman as the earth coupled with the idea of the earth as an active principle is a turnabout from the stock stereotypes that the woman, as "wife" and as "mother," as "weeping Madonna," or the "black goddess black hope black strength- / black mother" to quote Lorde in "Need: A Choral of Black Women's Voices" (Chosen Poems, 114), is a long-suffering rock of stability simply enduring her unchangeably horrible circumstance. Earth as an actor with her own mind is a very old and pagan idea that peeks through lines of the Lesbian poets, like the brook burbling in Aphrodite's living altar in Sappho's experience. Earth as female consciousness appears in my She Who poems, written in 1972, as a volcano who is a "woman of strong purpose" and, much more playfully, in the limerick:

She Whose skin is pitted with tiny holes
filled them up with microscopic moles,
who multiplied so quickly she was led
to fill them up with prairie dogs instead.
("She Who Poems," Work of a Common Woman, 95)

In "a plainsong from an older woman to a younger woman," the speaker asks herself to remember:

```
was I not        ruling
guiding naming
was I not        brazen
crazy    chosen
```

even the *stones* would do my bidding?
(105)

Among other things, this is a reference to the ancient story that women in ancient Egypt sang the pyramid stones into place with their voices and a special magical instrument. In this poem the older woman speaker asserts herself completely, "I am the will," she says, "and the riverbed." That the riverbed has a will has not been a Western idea. But it is an idea completely essential to the reclamation by women of our own powers.

The new island is being built of living rocks, as alive as apples, and as quickly as we can uncover them in our own lives:

The land that I grew up on is a rock

From my mother, a rock,
I have learned that rocks give
most of all.
What do rocks do? They hold the
forces of the earth together and
give direction . . .

They are like bone, the rocks. They frame.
They remain. They hold you.
They grind together to make digestible dirt . . .

the center of a rock, particularly
the one we live on,
is molten like a star, the core
is light,
enlightening, giving of
Intelligence[37]

In taking the Lesbian—and by extension, every woman—out of the realm of the exotic and placing her in the ordinary and everyday, woman with all her powers becomes central rather than extreme. What she has in common with herself and with other women becomes more important than what she is that is different from men. The new island of centrality, the centrality that is constructed of what is held in common, is of prime importance to the redefining being done by Lesbian poets.

The definition of *place* itself has been central to what we have done, as Lorde asked for a named tree in the place where we are. The first overtly Lesbian poem I wrote began "in the place where / her breasts come together" and continued "in the place where / her legs come together" (*Work of a Common Woman*, 42). Those were the most taboo, the most highly charged places forbidden for me to speak of—until then.

The first woman-owned and -run bookstore of our current feminist era was named by its Lesbian/feminist founders "A Woman's Place," the entire phrase being "A Woman's Place Is in the World." They consciously envisioned their bookstore as a place for women to come, alternative to the constriction of the home as well as of the workplace, and of the forbidden, dangerous streets. One of the first Lesbian novels of the 1970s era was *A Place for*

Us, the original title of Isabel Miller's *Patience and Sarah*. Even *Rubyfruit Jungle* is making reference to a location, being a takeoff on the term "Blackboard Jungle." All these references to place helped push Lesbianism out into the world, a hostile world at times, to be sure, a "jungle," but nevertheless we were perceived and perceiving ourselves as out of the house, out of confinement. In our lives, we have felt greatly without place, and continually out of place.

Audre Lorde, speaking about the alienation brought about by racism, sexism, and the great difficulty of Lesbian parenthood, wrote these wrenching lines in "School Note":

> My children play with skulls
> and remember
> for the embattled
> there is no place
> that cannot be
> home
> nor is.
> ("School Note," *The Black Unicorn*, 55)

"Home" for Lorde is an embattled place, not certainly in the sense of her own close-knit home—but in the sense of the Black Lesbian poet mother (and all she represents) out in the world. Apples are not the fruit of choice in Lorde's imagery; she is not writing from a European folk-tradition (as I am and Broumas is, for instance). Solidly based in the area of Manhattan and the modern world of urban Black America, Lorde draws additionally from the Barbadian birthland of both her parents, and also (especially in *The Black Unicorn* and her novel *Zami*) from West Africa and the Yoruba/Macumba traditions. Her island is real, contemporary, as much as it is historical. It is the Caribbean Island of Grenada, lost to her as a child of immigrants from it, as all our parents' lands are lost to us; lost again and more forcefully (though never permanently) in the degraded invasion of tiny Grenada by the US military in 1983.

The fruits in Lorde's work are fruits that bring women together, bring about the wholeness of spirit necessary for "women's power" to centralize itself. The fruits are tropical, avocados and mangoes mashed tantalizingly and licked from the belly by the (woman) lover; ripe banana planted in the beloved's "flower," spicy nutmeg (Grenada grows nutmeg as a primary crop) is ground like deep unspeakable emotions and thoughts in her mother's mortar, as the adolescent girl-poet watches in pain and wonder and desire. The ideal "place" of power in Lorde's work is in the act of women's bonding, a tie that does not always happen, and never happens easily. There are no facile answers in her complex imagery.

Again and again the contemporary Lesbian poets have stated the necessity of wholeness and integration as the way to a place, to home, and to the fruit of a new world. The Lesbian poet, through her Gay cultural traditions, through the poetic traditions to which she is heir through her art, and through her experiences as a woman—in some instances as a woman with an alive ethnic tribal cultural tradition as well—such Lesbian poets have a memory of an island, a world, "a planet," as H.D. called it, as she called Sappho herself, far different from life in this current industrialized world. Such Lesbian poets have the understanding that each woman is her own Muse, and in so doing we can find our sense of place with each other.

The nature of "place" is female, that is, the word derived from the female body, from "placenta," the place where the fetus is joined to its uterine home. "Who is your mother?" is the question, according to Paula Gunn Allen, of prime importance to the Pueblo Indian world; location in your mother's house is what gives you your sense of place in the social world.[38] "Location" is a similar idea as "placenta," being related to the same root as "lochial," meaning "birthing," as in "lochial blood." The way home for women is the way to ourselves.

When a woman is one with herself, is reunited after being fragmented from the female world, she is also reunited with her sense of place, with *place* itself. And in seeing herself as the Muse, herself as an active principle, she may also see the earth as an active principle. She sees it as a living apple, rather than an inert substance to be manipulated from without, or to render inspiration to "others." When the woman unites with the female in the universe she feels it inside of herself. "What do I have / if not my 2 hands & my apples," I wrote on occasion of losing my place in a community, and much of my sense of identity (*Work of a Common Woman*, 69). Olga Broumas, in a beautiful poem of a daughter uniting with her mother:

> Like two halves
> of a two-colored apple—red
> with discovery, green with fear— we lay
> ... Defenseless
> and naked as the day
> I slid from you

twin voices keening and the cord
pulsing our common protest, I'm coming back
back to you
woman, flesh
of your woman's flesh, your fairest, most
faithful mirror,
                    My love
transversing me like a filament
wired to the noonday sun.
("Snow White," *Beginning with O*, 70–71)

When a woman unites with the female in the universe she feels it inside of herself, and she perceives its willful powers, as Sappho must also, when she prayed to those powers to aid her in her purposes:

> *Let your (graceful form appear) near me (while I pray), lady Hera . . . now (be gracious and help me) in accordance with that ancient precedent.* (*Greek Lyric*, 69)

Lesbian poetry leads itself to its own foundations, and to this idea: the universe is alive, is a place, and we can unite with it; in fact it is essential that we do so. We can build a place for ourselves in it, so long as we understand the stones to be each other; we can reach our long-held apple, the one Sappho held back on the highest branch for us. This is a profoundly feminist and a profoundly poetic and a profoundly Lesbian idea.

II:
WRITING FROM A
HOUSE OF WOMEN

And Sappho said this:

Hither now, tender Graces and lovely-haired Muses.[1]

And this:

Stand (before me), if you love me, and spread abroad the grace that is on your eyes (155).

Sappho wrote from the base of Lesbianism, of bonded women in an intact culture, who had common understandings, a common mythological framework, a shared religion. She was central to her culture, and even in fragments has been central as a poet in Western culture as it has developed over twenty-five centuries.

Once an Alexandrian poet named Meleager referred to Sappho as "little—but all roses." The poet closest in quality to Sappho in the twentieth century, H.D., disagreed not only that she was "little," but also that "roses" was an apt description for the centrality of her position in her own world. In her essay "The Wise Sappho," H.D. wrote of her as:

Not roses, but an island, a country, a continent, a planet, a world of emotion, differing entirely from any present day imaginable world of emotion; a world of emotion that could only be imagined by the greatest of her own countrymen in the greatest period of that country's glamour, who themselves confessed her beyond their reach, beyond their song, not a woman, not a goddess even, but a song or the spirit of a song.

A song, a spirit, a white star that moves across the heaven to mark the end of a world epoch or to presage some coming glory.[2]

Sappho wrote *from* the context of a women's community, or what could be termed a "House of Women," into the context of her society at large. As a poet of her whole society, she wrote stories illustrative of the doings of the gods, male, female, masculine, feminine, or a mixture; wrote instructions for the appropriate behavior with respect to the gods and to human society; and she wrote wedding songs, as well as the overtly Lesbian love lyrics for which she is so famed and ill-famed, for which her work was burnt and partially submerged. In everything that remains of what she did, she maintained a female-based point of view, a women's collective center from which to speak of life and death, of beauty and love in general. She used an internal, subjective voice in an objective, public manner.

Sappho used clear, precise description and example to illustrate her points, drawing from the religious mythology and stories which were well understood as metaphors, as instructions of ordering the universe by the people of her time. So to give example of her love for a certain woman, Anactoria, she drew on the story of Queen Helen:

> Some say a host of cavalry, others of infantry, and others of ships, is the most beautiful thing on the black earth, but I say it is whatsoever a person loves. It is per-

fectly easy to make this understood by everyone: for she who far surpassed mankind in beauty, Helen left her most noble husband and went sailing off to Troy with no thought at all for her child or dear parents, but (love) led her astray . . . lightly . . . (and she?) has re-minded me now of Anactoria who is not here; I would rather see her lovely walk and the bright sparkle of her face than the Lydians' chariots and armed infantry . . . impossible to happen . . . mankind . . . but pray to share . . . unexpectedly. (Greek Lyric, 67)

As Helen loved Paris, so do I love you, Anactoria, she said in a very socialized and external voice. She often used a subjective internal voice as well, and H.D. felt that voice is the one we love most about her:

The gods, it is true, . . . are mentioned in these poems but at the end, it is for the strange almost petulant little phrases that we value this woman, this cry (against some simple unknown girl) of skirts and ankles we might think unnecessarily petty, yet are pleased in the thinking of it, or else the outbreak against her own intimate companions brings her nearer our own over-sophisticated, nerve-wracked era: "The people I help most are the most unkind," "O you forget me," or "You love someone better," "You are nothing to me," nervous, trivial tirades. Or we have in sweetened mood so simple a phrase "I sing"—not to please any god, goddess, creed or votary of religious rite—I sing not even in abstract contemplation, trance-like, remote from life, to please myself, but says this most delightful and friendly woman, "I sing and I sing beautifully like this, in order to please my friends—my girl friends." ("The Wise Sappho," 60)

It is this wholeness of itself that has given Sappho's work such value, and so much power as to keep the little scattered phrases vibrant and meaningful. In spite of tremendous opposition, deliberate misinterpretation, branding of her person as a moral degenerate, and the transformation of society over twenty-five hundred years' time, the words speak strong and clear today. She spoke of and to the gods, in her own personal voice, undistanced from them. In so doing, she spoke into the most collective consciousness of her culture without omitting her own personal consciousness. She spoke from a whole way of being, not an alienated, fragmented one; she spoke not as an outcast, but as someone at the very heart and center of her culture and of her times.

Her place was on an island, from what can be imagined as a "House of Women" in the middle of her world. This is a place of far more power than any of the descriptive titles and names modern people have tried to put to what she did. She was far more than a priestess in a religion of Aphrodite, teacher to daughters of a dying gynarchy, salon-hostess to a bevy of active artists or just a lyre-playing Lesbian with a lot of sexy friends. She wrote from such an integrated place as we modern women have only begun to imagine.

Even in the sparse fragments that remain, the names of her lovers and cohorts in the group around her are many, and her usual attitude toward them is instructive and descriptive praise:

I bid you, Abanthis, take (your lyre?) and sing of Gongyla, while desire once again flies around you, the lovely one—for her dress excited you when you saw it, and I rejoice (Greek Lyric, 73)

Sardis . . . often turning her thoughts in this direction . . . (she honoured) you as being like a goddess for all to see and took most delight in your song. Now she stands out among Lydian women like the rosy-fingered moon after sunset, surpassing all the stars, and its light spreads alike over the salt sea and the flowery fields; the dew is shed in beauty, and roses bloom and tender chervil and flowery melilot. (121)

H.D. has given us her own succinct descriptions of these women who formed such a constant and vital matrix of presence in Sappho's work, in "The Wise Sappho."

I love to think of Atthis and Andromeda curled on a sun-baked marble bench like the familiar Tanagra group, talking it over. What did they say? What did they think? Doubtless, they thought little or nothing and said much.

There is another girl, a little girl. Her name is Cleis. It is reported that the mother of Sappho was named Cleis. It is said that Sappho had a daughter whom she called Cleis . . . I see her heaping shells, purple and rose-edged, stained here and there with saffron colours, shells from Adriatic waters heaped in her own little painted bowl and poured out again and gathered up only to be spilt once more across the sands. We have seen Atthis of yester-year; An-

dromeda of "fair requital," Mnasidika with pro-
voking length of over-shapely limbs; Gyrinno, loved
for some appealing gesture or strange resonance of
voice or skill of fingertips, though failing in the es-
sential and more obvious qualities of beauty; Eran-
na with lips curved contemptuously over slightly
irregular though white and perfect teeth; angry
Eranna who refused everyone and bound white
violets only for the straight hair she herself braided
with precision and cruel self-torturing neatness
about her own head. We know of Gorgo, over-riotous,
too heavy, with special intoxicating sweetness, but
exhausting, a girl to weary of, no companion, her
over-soft curves presaging early development of
heavy womanhood.

Among the living there are these and others. Ti-
mas, dead among the living, lying with lily wreath
and funeral torch, a golden little bride, lives though
sleeping more poignantly even than the famous
Graeco-Egyptian beauty the poet's brother married at
Naucratis. Rhodope, a name redolent (even though
we may no longer read the tribute of the bride-
groom's sister) of the heavy out-curling, over-
lapping petals of the peerless flower. (65–66)

Obviously Sappho had a group around her; in fact, she
would later be called a whore for having so many women
lovers in her life. From all appearances, they constituted
a "community" to themselves, for some period of their
lives at least. She seems to have kept track of them even
when they had left her company, and often it appears they
left her company only to go to that of another woman,

women known as "Sappho's rivals." This is an interpretation based on a belief that women's relationships consist of either/or competition. In the Lesbian community as it exists in modern times, a "rival" may also be one's best friend, ex-lover, or lover-to-be, and the operation of jealousy is not so simple as it seems. Jealousy and other strong emotions, as well as love and desire, have to do with maintaining a network of Lesbians who support each other long after, or prior to, or in spite of never having been, lovers with each other.

For though Lesbian communities have been reduced since Sappho's time to a public example of two lovers, as in Gertrude and Alice, or one lonely Emily Dickinson pining after her brother's wife, such isolation is only public. The matrix underlying all Lesbian love is extensive and involves a group effort, and some sort of network of support from other women—women who are not necessarily Lesbian.

With the decline of the gynarchic states that set the stage for a poet such as Sappho in the first place, the community of women as a public force declined. It cloistered, and it survived in informal networks. It surfaced for several decades in the South of France during the twelfth century in concert with the women troubadours and other Gay and woman-centered social elements. After the women troubadours lived there, that area was a center of widespread heresy in the thirteenth century, heresy that encouraged female as well as Gay leadership, the worship of a two-sided deity, Gay and other libertarian sexual customs. The language of the troubadours is rich with imagery from the women's domain, of roses and hearts, chalices, and utter devotion to ideals and to love. But this movement was warred upon and swept under by the heavy hand of the Inquisition. Vestiges of a public women's community went underground with the whores, witches, Lesbians, and other fairy people.

In the nineteenth century, Emily Dickinson, isolated spinster *par excellence*, had the presence of other women in her life and their dedication saved her work from extinction. Her friendly editor, Thomas Higginson, treated her like an exotic pet, did not really like her work, and discouraged her from publishing it, although that seems to have been what she wanted more than anything. After her death, it was the women related to her who put her poems into print. They managed to do this despite their fear of disclosing the sheer overtness of Emily's Lesbian feelings, which almost caused sister-in-law Sue Dickinson to destroy the packets of hand-written manuscripts. The packets were literally saved by Emily's faithful younger sister Lavinia. In trying to edit the controversial material decades after it was written, Sue's daughter, Martha Dickinson Bianchi, censored the Lesbian references from Dickinson's letters and poems before publishing very bland renditions of the poet's actual sentiments. But in spite of their difficulties with the overtly Lesbian and more sharp-tongued parts, they retained her work and they made it public, even in the absence of a real women's community.

And then, astoundingly, as the twentieth century opened, it all began to re-form: a vocally growing feminism, the open expression and development of a Lesbian community, and a public expression of the centrality of women to themselves. With Amy Lowell and her lover Ada Russell, this expression took the form of a coterie of Lesbian friends who kept in contact with each other, visited each other, influenced each other. They also had tremendous impact on twentieth century ideas and literature. This network of friends included H.D. and the novelist Bryher, who had a covert Lesbian marriage and child-rearing arrangement together, though the image projected by and about H.D. is that she was ambivalent about Lesbianism. She continually idealized male lovers; she was uncertain enough about being taken seriously as the brilliant female intelligence that she was that she used as a pen name her initials, H.D., instead of her name Hilda Doolittle. But she spent the greater portion of her adult life—more than forty years—in relation to Bryher; Bryher was her island from which she wrote. The main body of her work is a deep, intense exploration of women's powers, couched in metaphoric structures drawn from classical Greek mythology and the Egyptian occult tradition.

Other early-twentieth-century Lesbian writers who followed on Dickinson's Victorian/Calvinist heels were able to be openly or at least semi-openly Lesbian in the company of other poets, could even form a social group with them. So the very dykish Lowell stayed influential with the Imagist movement that included Ezra Pound, D.H. Lawrence, and William Carlos Williams, as well as H.D. And the very dykely novelist Bryher, though she apparently had a terrible reputation among the men as a termagant and other frighteningly "butch" things, was at least moderately acceptable to H.D.'s peers in the literary society so vital to all of their work.

Gertrude Stein, in her beautiful and outrageous Caesar haircut, is most well-known for her position among prominent male artists of the century, but she and Alice were also part of a network of Lesbian friends. Those dinner parties, of course, did not receive public attention, yet they happened; I dare say they were sustaining.

Networks of contemporary women sustain Lesbian writers, and the writers themselves look to their own heritage for food and drink and direction. Dickinson had certainly read Sappho, though she was most directly and deeply influenced by Elizabeth Barrett Browning. Amy Lowell expressed fierce loyalty to the women poets who had gone before her. Jean Gould, in her biography *Amy: The World of Amy Lowell and the Imagist Movement*, wrote this description of Lowell's devotion to her sister writers:

> Her poem, "The Sisters," opening with a meditation on the "family" of women poets, was published in the *North American Review*. This was the poem in which she stated her views on the "queer lot" they were . . . In "The Sisters" she paid tribute to three poets she much admired. Of "Sapho" she said: "And she is Sapho— Sapho—not Miss or Mrs." But the next poet, "Mrs. Browning," of whom she is very fond, she would never dream of calling "Ba," and says bitterly, ". . . as if I didn't know / What those years felt like tied down to the sofa. / Confounded Victoria, and the slimy inhibitions she loosed on all us Anglo-Saxon creatures!" The third "sister," Emily . . . Dickinson, she could not bring herself to address as "Miss Dickinson," or send a formal visiting card; in her fantasy meeting with Emily, she "climbed over the fence, and found her deep / Engrossed in the

doing of a humming-bird / Among nasturtiums."
She called Emily a "Frail little elf, / The lonely brain-
child of a gaunt maturity," who "hung her womanhood
upon a bough / And played ball with the stars—too
long— too long long— / Until at last she lost even
the desire / To take it down." Amy blamed not only
Queen Victoria again, but also Martin Luther, "And
behind him the long line of Church Fathers / Who
draped their prurience like a dirty cloth / About the
naked majesty of God."[3]

The connections of contemporary Lesbian poets to
each other, though they may have developed late, are of
vital importance to the growth of our ideas. Of the con-
temporary Lesbian poets under discussion, Adrienne
Rich has written about H.D., Dickinson, Lowell, Stein,
Lorde, and myself. Olga Broumas has credited Sappho and
Rich (along with Sylvia Plath, Anne Sexton, and Virginia
Woolf); Allen has written about my work and Lorde's;
with this essay I have now written about, and do hereby
credit as influences, all of them, beginning about 1977,
except for Lorde, whose work I was beginning to know
and utterly love by 1971.[4] And Parker of course, whose vi-
tal lines I knew from 1970 and have written about, as she
also mentioned me in her writings and exchanged intense
letters with Lorde. And Stein, whose words were with
me since childhood. I am saying all these names as a way
of showing a lineage, and how conscious it has been. We
have consciously drawn from a tradition leading back to
Sappho and to a House of Women whether we have called
it that or not.

Writing from a House of Women Out into the World

The decision an artist makes, to speak for women and to speak as a woman (and likewise as a member of any group, a Lesbian, Jewish, Black, working class, transgender, disabled, or otherwise marginalized person, etc.) is probably the most powerful decision she will make. For in making it, she chooses autonomy, she chooses to stand somewhere in particular to speak out to her society. Her work, in locating itself so specifically socially and historically, takes on a power it cannot have if she chooses, instead, to speak anonymously, "universally." But having made this choice, she faces another danger, for if she addresses only members of her special groups, her work will have limited power, and limited integrity. It is the acknowledgment and then the inclusion of all our selves that leads us to the idea of life as consisting of many expanding, multicultural worlds in which everyone is ultimately included (as well as excluded).

This expansion happens after the artist plants herself in the midst of all her groups and embraces the cultural separatism that enables autonomy, self-definition, and community to develop. From this strong home base, then, she can approach the world at large as somebody in particular, as Sappho did when she bragged that no one could out-sing the poets of Lesbos.

If the network, or base of women bonded as friends, is home base for the Lesbian poets, it is not for its own sake only. It has not been for the purpose of aggrandizing Lesbianism, nor even of "making the world a safer place" for Lesbianism (though that is sometimes a necessary effect). Rather it has been a place from which to speak and a lens through which to view our society at large. It is paradoxically both a central and an "outsider" position from which to take a stance.

In finding an appropriate voice with which to speak from her own highly eccentric dykely life, Amy Lowell was drawn to and highly influential within what Ezra Pound named the "Imagist movement" of poetry. Imagism is poetry in which romantic sludge and conventional metaphor, rhyme schemes, and taken-for-granted ideas were stripped away, sheared off to leave a crisp emphasis on the image alone, the image itself, to convey meaning. This left the mind's eye free to make new connections, free of nineteenth-century values. The Imagists, and Amy Lowell in particular, looked to the literature of American Indians, especially Pueblo Indians, who she openly imitated in a series of poems. She also drew from early Chinese and Japanese forms to find a distillation of line and thought, a spareness of obvious truth. In her very ambitious and productive way Lowell was so busy an organizer of the Imagist movement and supporter of the other Imagist writers that Pound later, and in disgust, called it the "Amigist movement."

Lowell concentrated her artistic energies on stripping the poem to a clean, spare image, on writing in almost terse, "Americanized" poetic sentences, though still keeping to schemes of rhyme and rhythm that were relatively tight (compared to Whitman, who had opened sentences to loquacious freedom forty years earlier). Lowell began using coarse, startling, formerly unacceptable phrases, descriptions, and ideas. The Harvard society of her father and brothers found the lines in her poem "Grotesque" to be insulting: "Why do the lillies goggle their tongues at me / . . . / Why do they shriek your name / And spit at me" (Gould, 180).

Not that she didn't wax beautifully lyrical much of the time, especially in her love poems to Ada. In "Song for a Viola d'Amore," she writes:

The lady of my choice is bright
As a clematis at the touch of night,
As a white clematis with a purple heart
When twilight cuts the earth and sun apart[5]

"Patterns" is virtually the only poem of Lowell's to have been so heavily anthologized as to keep her name alive today, when her work is out of print and difficult to find. In this poem, she translated the social strictures and pressures she felt on her own Lesbian life into a poem about a woman who is buttoned into the whalebone and brocade of rigid social convention. The woman walks in a lush, promising, and sensual garden with her male lover, unable to give herself over to her passion though she is able to fantasize a naked embrace with him. As the poem proceeds, we see that she is reading a letter announcing that the lover has been killed in battle, and all their careful adherence to sexual strictures has been for nothing. The poem's ending line, "Christ! what are patterns for," combines a bitter curse, a naming of the responsible party, and a crying out to god, all at one time. The words still shock, and in 1915 they were considered extremely coarse language for a poet, let alone an upper-class lady poet, to use.

The emotional substance of "Patterns" came from her own life with Ada Russell, and from the social restrictions they felt about being a queer couple. Jean Gould says in her biography that after writing "Patterns" the poet was "so buoyant over achieving exactly the effect she desired that she could hardly wait for Ada's opinion, and she met her at the door with it when her friend came home" (Gould, 180–81).

In "Patterns," Amy was writing out from a base of Lesbian love, out from it into the world at large, translating her own experience into terms a wide and heterosexual audience could instantly identify with. In so doing, she spoke against all moral strictures, for all who wanted to break with Victorian morality, for all who understood that the sexual inhibitions had something to do with the "pattern called war."

"Imagism" set up a form of new lyricism that H.D. fully developed after her early "Imagist" years. She turned to an astonishing, breathtaking epic poetry, where she explored epic themes in tight, precise, lyric couplets. The pairing together of the two forms was essential for her task of writing modern mythic-occult-prophetic-historic-epics from *within* a woman's point of view. With her form, H.D., like Sappho, is able to portray both the inside world and the outside world: both the narrative of what happened and the inner dialogue of what the experience felt, looked, tasted, smelled like. In her form, she married the feminine/lyric/Sapphic and the masculine/epic/narrative/Homeric. She reversed their effects: the usually "objective" narration of events is focused on an internal/occult landscape:

Clytemnestra gathered the red rose,
Helen, the white,

but they grew on one stem,
one branch, one root in the dark;
I have not answered his question,
which was the veil?
which was the dream?
was the dream, Helen upon the ramparts?
was the veil, Helen in Egypt?[6]

The usually cold external narrative is told in a warm, lyric, personal voice; yet the story being told is epic, is history:

Be still, I say, strive not,
yourself to annul the decree;
you can not return to the past

nor stay the sun in his course;
be still, I say, why weep?
you spoke of your happiness,

I was near you and heard you speak;
I heard you question Achilles
and Achilles answer you;

be still, O sister, O shadow;
your sister, your shadow was near,
lurking behind the pillars,

counting the fall of your feet,
as Achilles beneath the ramparts;
you spoke and I heard you speak;
(103)

Perhaps only a woman who loved both women and men in her life could have accomplished, or would have attempted, such a wedding of forms, forms that have been considered oppositional.

Turning the Inside Outside: Gertrude Stein

A classic dyke in form and function, Gertrude Stein sat with the male artists and intellectuals who visited the home she and Alice Toklas kept in Paris. She did not sit with the wives of the artists; she was a woman who crossed over into a man's world of writing and innovating literature. "I will come back a lion," she said of her move to Europe, and she meant a literary lion, not a pussy cat. And perhaps Alice did not want her to sit with the wives, and be subject to their flirting. Alice, after all, was the wife of an artist too, an artist named Gertrude, though unlike those other wives, Toklas's name is remembered. Women were the main subject of Stein's art; she wrote of them in portraits and stories, myths and poems, using humor, sensitivity, sensuality, commentary, description. She wrote *as* a woman of her times, using an interior women's landscape. Mundane domestic objects and scenes were her field of study: furniture, pictures, cows, poodles, people at dinner, people in love, people talking together. For Stein, the House of Women was her own house, and her own Lesbian perspective on the nature of the house, as she developed it in the close companionship she shared with Toklas.

Gertrude Stein's lifelong preoccupation included translating the everyday personal experience of a woman-to-woman relationship into a literature that no longer overtly contains this taboo experience yet covertly contained it in great detail. In gaining the ability to put into her work the love between herself and Alice Toklas, she not only stripped poetry to the spare image, she also stripped away image and entered the architecture of language itself. In that domain she began perceiving and treating words as individual bricks that have a free-floating meaning of their own, unattached to the automatic cliched meanings they have in sentence form.

By detaching verbs from nouns, by detaching linear plot from language, taking apart the old formula that noun acts upon object and verb is amplified by adverb, she opened up the nature of language itself, made spaces in it. Into these spaces of free floating or uncliched meaning, she dropped the substance and the everyday happenings of her life with Alice, including their erotic life, their pet names for each other, and their highly personal ways of being together. She did this with such subtlety that only one poem was considered overtly homosexual enough to be included in the *Penguin Book of Homosexual Verse*:

I love my love with a v
Because it is like that
I love my love with a b
Because I am beside that
A king.
I love my love with an a
Because she is a queen
I love my love and a a is the best of them
Think well and be a King,
Think more and think again
I love my love with a dress and a hat

I love my love and not with this or with that
I love my love with a y because she is my bride
I love her with a d because she is my love beside
Thank you for being there
Nobody has to care
Thank you for being here
Because you are not there.
     And with and without me which is and without she
                      she
   can be late
and then and how and all around we think and found that
                   it
  is time to cry
  she and I.[7]

Stein opened up language itself, the very bricks of it, the very *of* of it, the *it* of it, the *the* of *of* with lines like these: "With it which it as it if it is to be to be to come to in which to do in that place."[8] Or this one: "When is and thank and is and and and is when is when is and when thank when is and when and thank" (113).

Amy Lowell and the Imagists had freed poetry of the sultry, stultifying imagery of the Victorian age in order to allow for a more "modern" content—and in Lowell's case at least, a more Lesbian content. Gertrude Stein redid the structure of the language itself. She collapsed into one voice the two supposedly oppositional extremes of perception—objective and subjective—collapsed them into one form, one technique, one mode of understanding. The result is a truer form of objectivity, a virtually value-free language, as well as an almost ego-free and sentiment-free experience of the subjectivity.

By equalizing the value of each word, Stein was locating the commonness of language, the equality of value each word has with every other. She created each word as a unit of meaning in and of itself, making the meaning new each time from the context of the other words around it, and also from the multitude of associations we make in our inner brains, in our word-poetic minds of simple association. For example, try reading aloud this line: "With it which it as it if it is to be to be to come to in which to do in that place" (109). Or this one: "When is and thank and is and and and is when is when is and when thank when is and when and thank" (113).

In exploring this equalizing terrain, she freed language from its linear plot. Not only did she free the image from the old romantic affiliations as Lowell and the Imagists did, but she also freed each sentence from its linear plot of grammar: subject is a noun acting with a verb upon a subject and is modified by adjectives. She made nouns out of articles and verbs out of nouns and subjects out of adverbs and conjunctions. And in so doing she took all the moral judgmentalness from language, all the expectation: hero saves heroine from evil landlord. She removed all the expectation: this is good, this is bad, this is indifferent. In her sentences each word is indifferent, is good and is bad. Each word is evil, is a landlord, a heroine, is saving. And so she was able to use the substance of her inner life, her home life, her personal life and those of all her friends, not merely the socially acceptable ones. And because she had freed the language of all possible judgment there is no way to read her work and to judge her life in any terms except her own. It takes a very wild and major lion to do this, to set the terms of value, to the art.

Consider this passage from "Lifting Belly":

Lifting belly with me.
You inquire.
What you do then.
Pushing.
Thank you so much.
And lend a hand.
What is lifting belly now.
My baby.
Always sincerely.
Lifting belly says it there.
Thank you for the cream.
Lifting belly tenderly.
A remarkable piece of intuition.
I have forgotten all about it.
Have you forgotten all about it.
Little nature which is mine.
Fairy ham
Is a clam.
Of chowder
Kiss him Louder.
Can you be especially proud of me.
Lifting belly a queen.
In that way I can think.
Thank you so much.
I have,
lifting belly for me.
I can not forget the name.
lifting belly for me.
Lifting belly again.
Can you be proud of me.

I am
Then we say it.
In miracles.
Can we say it and then sing. You mean drive.
I mean drive.
We are full of pride.
Lifting belly is proud.
Lifting belly is my queen.
Lifting belly happy.
Lifting belly see.
lifting belly.
Lifting belly address.
Little washers.
Lifting belly how do you do.
Lifting belly is famous for recipes.
You mean Genevieve.
I mean I never ask for potatoes.
But you liked them then.
And now.
Now we know about water.
Lifting belly is a miracle.
And the Caesars.
The Caesars are docile.
Not more docile than is right.
No beautifully right.
And in relation to a cow.
And in relation to a cow.
Do believe me when I incline.
You mean obey.
I mean obey.
Obey me.
Husband obey your wife.
Lifting belly is so dear.

To me.
Lifting belly is smooth,
Tell lifting belly about matches.
Matches can be struck with the thumb.
Not by us.
No indeed.
What is it I say about letters.
Twenty six.
And counted.
And counted deliberately.
This is not as difficult as it seems.
Lifting belly is so strange.
And quick.
Lifting belly in a minute.
Lifting belly in a minute now.
In a minute.
Not to-day.
No not to-day.
Can you swim.
Lifting belly can perform aquatics.
Lifting belly is astonishing.
Lifting belly for me.
Come together.
Lifting belly near.
I credit you with repetition.
Believe me I will not say it.
And retirement.
I celebrate something.
Do you.

(45–47)

Looking at the outside from the inside and at the inside from the outside, Stein fulfilled her function of Lesbian poet to the highest degree. She also achieved a singular objectivity with this method, especially about highly charged social stigmas. After shelving as unpublishable her first, and completely Lesbian, novel of a triangle of young women, she proceeded to write *Three Lives*, three portraits of women very different from herself and from each other. The first of these, "Melanctha," is a rare example in literature of a white author writing of Black characters simply for themselves, and, like the Lesbians in her first novel, portrayed solely in relation to each other rather than to the outside (and white) world. However, Stein's racial bias also was made clear in her equating of some of the "good" qualities of Melanctha to white qualities.

From her early and relatively concrete, linear works ("Melanctha" has a recognizable plot, for instance) she continued to experiment more and more with the nature of language, thought and communication itself. In *The Making of Americans* (of which it is joked that only Toklas, who typed it, has read the whole thing), and in her erotic poems such as "Lifting Belly," and even more in her later plays, she treated language as a real being, plastic rather than fixed. Her language creates context rather than being contextual. She was exploring the neurological impressions and connections words make inside our brains. Modern psychologists, also being, as Stein was earlier, students of the great psychologist William James, would do this themselves in developing behaviorism and neurolinguistics.

Concerning naming, she said, very specifically:

So then in "Tender Buttons" I was making poetry but and it seriously troubled me, dimly I knew that nouns made poetry but in prose I no longer needed the help of nouns and in poetry did I need the help of nouns. Was there not a way of naming things that would not invent names, but mean names without naming them.

I had always been very impressed from the time that I was very young by having had it told me and then afterwards feeling it myself that Shakespeare in the forest of Arden had created a forest without mentioning the things that make a forest. You feel it all but he does not name its names . . .

I commenced trying to do something in Tender Buttons about this thing. I went on and on trying to do this thing. I remember in writing An Acquaintance with Description looking at anything until something that was not the name of that thing but was in a way that actual thing would come to be written.

Naturally, and one may say that is what made Walt Whitman naturally that made the change in the form of poetry, that we who had known the names so long did not get a thrill from just knowing them. We that is any human being living has inevitably to feel the thing anything being existing, but the name of that thing of which it is that anything is no longer anything to thrill anyone except children. So as everybody has to be a poet, what was there to do. This that I have just described, the creating it without naming it, was what broke the rigid form of the noun the simple noun poetry which now was broken.[9]

In collapsing the external and the internal into one view, lining them up on one single plane of being, she is using a technique similar to that used in Indigenous poetry, including the work of American Indian poets. She reversed the belief that so much Western writing and Western science has had: that one must and can choose between the internal and the external vision, can split them. (They are usually split artificially along gender lines, racial lines, and class lines.) But if we deny the internal, we cannot see the external very clearly either, and vice versa, although we can have the emotional illusion of clear perception. This is a culture trance, as Paula frequently called it, a mythic story all participants give as "reasons" for their feelings and behavior in any given situation.[10]

By unifying the internal and external viewpoints, and by assigning equal value to each component of her work, each letter of the word, each word of the sentence, each image being described, Stein enabled a powerful nonlinear and democratic landscape of the mind; she literally disenchanted the mythic "sleep," the "culture trance" or previous myths of Western patriarchal literature, and she did this primarily through her approach to language.

Toward a Contemporary Lesbian House of Women

For contemporary Lesbian poets who have undertaken a definition of the word "Lesbian" and its many implications, and who deliberately have established as large as possible a "house" of women based on bonding in the most essential ways, three major areas have concerned us. These are self-determination, autonomy, and community, the same concerns that preoccupy any group attempting to maintain its identity in a hostile environment.

All these qualities seem implicitly present in Sappho's work. Certainly she had a community of women around her, even whose names are known to us; she had vital importance to her culture, as her popularity attests; she had an intact ceremony, a mythos, from which to draw connection to the forces of the universe. Her definitions, like her gods, were her own.

"As for him who finds fault with us, may silliness and sorrow overtake him,"[11] goes one popular poster version of one of her fragments, but nothing indicates it was the woman-bonded culture she represented that anyone in her day would find fault with. Her words and definitions were hers, for her teaching, praying, and singing purposes, delivered outward from her societal position of woman-gendered centrality. An ancient writer named Demetrius said of her, "This is why when Sappho sings of beauty her words are beautiful and sweet; so too when she sings of loves and spring and the halcyon: every type of beautiful word is woven into her poetry, and some of them are her own creation" (Greek Lyric, 185).

The effort of establishing and re-confirming self-definition in the voices of the contemporary Lesbian poets has included reclaiming words with loaded, stereotypic content such as, Lesbian, dyke, whore, cunt, mother, daughter, birthing, and the like—and extending as a matter of the course of our lives into the other groups to which we also variously belong: Black, feminist, working class, Jewish, fat, literary, Indigenous, intellectual, alcoholic, leftist, mystic, revolutionary, immigrant, American. The effort of reconstructing a Lesbian self-definition also has included filling in the silences first pointed out by working-class and feminist writer Tillie Olsen and taken up by

Adrienne Rich in her essays and her book *On Lies, Secrets, and Silence*.

The leadership exerted by Lesbian and feminist poets as the mass movements of women developed during the 1970s cannot be exaggerated. Even well into the '80s, I can hardly walk into a women's center anywhere in the country without seeing lines from any of a dozen of my own and others' poems posted on the wall as mottoes of strength and inspiration to all who pass through. We have all been recorded, reproduced in all manner of media. and read by millions of women (and men). Audre Lorde's poetic political stances have become ethical guidelines in more than one sector, as have Pat Parker's and Adrienne Rich's.

Poets—both feminist and Lesbian, but especially Lesbian/feminist—have repeatedly surfaced with the key words and phrases that later became full-blown movement issues and obsessions. These have included many aspects of sexism and the belittling of women, details of homophobia and compulsory heterosexuality, rape, alcoholism and its debilitating effects on our lives, and racism between women, to use some more obvious examples. Sometimes the poets write out of group consciousness as it develops among active people around them; sometimes they speak from their own individual courage and integrity. Sometimes they have absorbed the ensuing attacks of doubt and hostility as the issue is argued into a public life of its own. Always they are operating as Sappho operated, as any true poet operates: defining the culture around her, giving it name, substance, and rhythm so it can grow into a full life.

The development of genuine autonomy has been undertaken by modern Lesbian feminists and given much attention by the poets. This has included stressing the necessity for women to begin, and to continue, looking to each other and to ourselves for our value and sense of esteem, looking to sameness and commonality for strength and motivation. Pat Parker, in the last stanza of a poem called "GROUP," names a major source of reclaimed self-love after it has been torn from us, in this case by racism as well as sexism and homophobia. After describing lessons she learned of hatred of herself for looking Black, and from being called bad, "I do have memory of teachers / you are heathens / why can't you be / like the white kids / you are bad—," she concluded:

> now
> there are new lessons
>   new teachers
> each week I go to my group
>   see women
>   Black women
> Beautiful Black Women
> & I am in love
>   with each of them
> & this is important
>   in the loving
> in the act of loving
>   each woman
> I have learned a new lesson
> I have learned
>   to love myself[12]

The Rise of the Common Woman

With the appearance of *The Common Woman Poems*, which I published in 1969 in a basement mimeograph machine edition, the Lesbian and all manner of other formerly exotic or overlooked women's experiences were placed—literarily speaking—in a framework of commonality and at the *center* of women's experience. "The common woman is as common as good bread, and will rise," the poems ended, and they were quoted and sloganized for over a million encounters in media that ranged from television to T-shirts to walls, from music to anthologies to names of women's enterprises.

Adrienne Rich commented that:

The 'Common Woman' is far more than a class description. What is 'common' in and to women is the intersection of oppression and strength, damage and beauty. It is, quite simply, the *ordinary* in women which will 'rise' in every sense of the word—spiritually and in activism. For us, to be 'extraordinary' or 'uncommon' is to fail. History has been embellished with 'extraordinary,' and 'exemplary,' 'uncommon,' and of course 'token' women whose lives have left the rest unchanged. The 'common woman' is in fact the embodiment of the extraordinary will-to-survive in millions of women, a life-force which transcends childbearing: unquenchable, chromosomic reality. Only when we can count on this force in each other, everywhere, know absolutely that it is there for us, will we cease abandoning and being abandoned by 'all of our lovers.'[13]

By placing one Lesbian portrait into a matrix of seven portraits of seven women, I was writing out of the Lesbian couple bond (influenced by the feminist movement) into a much larger world of women in general, who can be seen as and can act as a group based on their commonality, their common interest in improving their lives, and their common strengths of experience and heritage. The idea of common women passed on into Adrienne Rich's *The Dream of a Common Language* where it was greatly broadened by new phrases. The "Common Dream" was a common dream of women together, of the social implications and possibilities of the bond of women, to each other and to their own strengths and powers. This, she suggested, could be articulated by a common language, a "whole new poetry," called for in "Transcendental Etude."[14] By 1976, Olga Broumas would be confident enough about the possibility of a women's language to write:

A woman-made
language would
have as many synonyms for pink
light-filled
holy as
the Eskimo does
for snow.[15]

Lesbian and feminist groups of all descriptions have used the word "common" in one capacity or another, to name stores, restaurants, health collectives, or newsletters and magazines, as Midwest Lesbians did with "Common Lives/Lesbian Lives." Lesbian poets have repeated the idea frequently: Olga Broumas mentions "common protest" in her poem "Snow White," and entering "into the common, suspended disbelief of love."[16] Poet Alice Bloch calls her life with her lover our "common life" in a bitter poem expressing lack of social acknowledgment and support for Lesbian relationships.[17]

One critic has pointed out the all-important difference between "universal" and "common" as it has been explored in my work and in Adrienne Rich's. "Common refers to that which is shared; that which no matter how incomplete, as life is incomplete, no matter how imperfect—essentially non-ideal—exists here, now, in its particularity as true." And again, "We do not lose ourselves to find ourselves, we *find* ourselves to find ourselves."[18] *Universal*, "one-world," implies everyone having to fit into one standard (and of course that one, that "uni," is going to turn out to be a white, male, heterosexual, young, educated, middle-class, etc., model). For if there can only be one model, how can it be otherwise? "Common" means many-centered, many overlapping islands of groups each of which maintains its own center and each of which is central to society for what it gives to society.

Critic Mary Carruthers has called my "She Who" poems a virtual book of common prayer for women,[19] and that was what I intended when I wrote the bulk of them over a nine-month period in 1972. At that time, the vision of commonality was solidifying into something both larger and smaller, but certainly more concrete. We were busy establishing a base of woman-controlled institutions that would begin to answer to the expressed needs of all kinds of women. Women were dramatically shifting the focus of their lives, entering the workforce, changing their family structures, bonding with and as different kinds of lovers than they had ever imagined for themselves, launching careers and starting businesses. Commonality gave way to community, the attempt to concretize the bonding of women into a group identity.

Not surprisingly, the "She Who" poems were written while I was living in a household consisting entirely of Lesbians—some forty of them living there during a five-year period. The "She Who" series ends with a list of "every kind of woman I could think of" and the imagery is not limited to the United States nor to women in the industrial state:

the woman who escaped from the jailhouse
the woman who is walking across the desert
the woman who buries the dead
the woman who taught herself writing
the woman who skins rabbits
the woman who believes her own word
the woman who chews bearskin
the woman who eats cocaine
the woman who thinks about everything
the woman who has the tattoo of a bird
the woman who puts things together
the woman who squats on her haunches
the woman whose children are all different   colors

singing   I am the will of the woman
                        the woman
                        my will is unbending

when She-Who-moves-the-earth will turn over
when She Who moves, the earth will turn over

("The woman whose head is on fire,"
                    Work of a Common Woman, 107–9)

In each case, I had a specific person in mind, someone I knew or had read about. For instance, "the woman whose children are all different colors" was in honor of Diane DiPrima, who I have always admired.

The kind of international connection present in the "She Who" series is vividly apparent in Audre Lorde's work. In the startling, physically charged love poem "Meet," the lovers are not only united with women in all parts of history—including the old ports of Palmyra and Abomey-Calavi through which enslaved people passed but also with the earth's own substance and the animal world, especially the lion family:

Woman when we met on the solstice
high over halfway between your world and mine
rimmed with full moon and no more excuses
your red hair burned my fingers as I spread you
tasting your ruff down to sweetness
and I forgot to tell you
I have heard you calling across this land
in my blood before meeting
and I greet you again
on the beaches in mines lying on platforms
in trees full of tail-tail birds flicking
and deep in your caverns of decomposed granite
even over my own laterite hills
after a long journey
licking your sons
while you wrinkle your nose at the stench.

Coming to rest
in the open mirrors of your demanded body
I will be black light as you lie against me
I will be heavy as August over your hair
our rivers flow from the same sea
and I promise to leave you again
full of amazement and our illuminations
dealt through the short tongues of color
or the taste of each other's skin as it hung
from our childhood mouths . . .

Taste my milk in the ditches of Chile and Ouagadougou
in Tema's bright port while the priestess of Larteh
protects us
in the high meat stalls of Palmyra and Abomey-Calavi
now you are my child and my mother
we have always been sisters in pain.

Come in the curve of the lion's bulging stomach
lie for a season out of the judging rain
we have mated we have cubbed
we have high time for work and another meeting
women exchanging blood
in the innermost rooms of moment
we must taste of each other's fruit
at least once
before we shall both be slain.[20]

Commonality means we get to belong to a number of overlapping groups, not just one. Audre Lorde's work speaks out of the experiences and urgent concerns of the Black community, which she uses as a base from which

to speak to the white community most critically of mur-
derous, neglectful, and defensive white racist behavior.
From the base of Lesbian/feminism she has been able to
speak critically of Black attitudes painful to her; and now
from her newest base of Black and Third World women,
including Lesbians, she is speaking critically of the treat-
ment of Black women by Black men in poems such as
"Need: A Choral for Black Women's Voices."[21] By stand-
ing in so many places, she is able to teach a philosophy
of wholeness, of all our splintered selves that need to be
brought together in love, in anger, in pain, in refusal to
lie, in listening, in desire, in greatness of thought, in com-
mon understandings.

The movement of the modern Lesbian poet has been
toward establishing a Woman's House of Power and Unity
from which to speak as a healing and critiquing voice, di-
rectly into each community of which we are a part—and
these are specific to each author and diverse from each
other.

Common Likeness, Common Difference

A most interesting development of the idea of com-
monality has appeared in the term "common differences":
defining and retaining racial and ethnic identities with-
out losing either our affinity as women and/or as Lesbians.
This means acknowledging that more than one island of
centrality exists, more than one "House of Women" is
operating. We can see this while still keeping the continual
underlying capacity to learn from, listen to and love, pro-
tect and support each other. This involves listening with

an open heart to *how* we differ, even inside a common structure. Knowing also, as Lorde has pointed out repeatedly, "other" is an aspect of ourselves projected.

"The Garden" from *Shadow Country* by Paula Gunn Allen is one of a number of poems that speaks directly into the idea of common differences:

scene i

sky still bright
we weed, companionable.
she on her side of the low wall
me on mine
"they leave their shells in the ground"
she says, "see these holes? I don't know
why, they have to be dug up and
thrown away." she holds up
a transparent thing,
tissue pattern for an insect dress.
her petunias, my com, beans, squash and I
nod amiably.

in the hills last night
two more animals
dismembered:
rectum, lip, nostril, vagina
split.
bodies left bloodless
on the unmarked grass.
something out there.
something unknown.
I straighten, groaning

wipe sweat from my eyes.
mystic impulse all around
slicing holes in air
digging bad dreams
in daylight.
sun like a corpse over me.
sky blooming deep.
a shroud.

scene ii

unmannered.
soft as night.
air keening.
sky building.
what manners these?
fear lightly easing itself over
back wall, through trees.
starshine
beginning at the edge.
her dress moves with ease, eyes
glitter, hair
so soft in evening wind, she
recalls summer nights,
arms like branches singing, body
sinking graceful into dusk.
comfort of lounge chair
holds buttocks, back, pliant neck.
she dreams of Pentecost, tongues
of flame above her shining hair,
to this place
a manner of speaking touches her lips

lightly, careful for her carelessness,
birds settle in for the night, crying.
daylight evaporates as she swirls
her drink, sips cold with perfect ease
against her teeth, rests against cushions
soft as dissolving clouds
overhead.
trees by the back wall
begin to stir
ominous
sky goes dark.
she doesn't see,
she doesn't make a sound.
Pentecost shimmers
flows from her hair
between her thighs.

scene iii

light angling
volunteer's face ashen
up two days and nights
starshine is not what
got in her eyes.
he used a knife
on her vagina she tells me,
and maybe the hatchet we found
beside the bed
the blood, my god, she tells me.
outside surgery we stand
uneasy, graceless, longing
for the carelessness of birds.

scene iv

haunted
tissue paper hulls
bad dreams in daylight
no sleep in dark
before my eye
a shadow
photograph of Brazilian Indian woman hung
by the ankles from a pole
long hair sweeping down
blowing in the laden breeze
white hunter standing next to her
spread legs. she is naked.
she is dead.[22]

"The Garden" is a particularly sharply drawn theme that is a familiar and unresolved one: the two women are placed in a garden, which is their commonality as women, with women's traditions. But the reality of what is happening there is entirely different for one than it is for the other. For the shadow woman there is ever-present horror, which she can never lose sight of, for she is never safe and never has the illusion of safety. For the comfortable woman there is obliviousness of danger, of the real nature of her neighbors, of even the nature of the insects in her little garden or the attacks on animals in the hills behind her house. She has the frivolity that results from ignorance and over-shelter. She does not have any idea what the Indigenous woman sees; and in this poem she makes no attempt to find out. So she is shut out from knowing the other's view of life, but she is also cut off from her own life as well, for one cannot live on petunias and dreams of beatitude. Yet in spite of the denial of the oblivious woman and her inability to acknowledge the danger, let alone protect, they are nevertheless in *fact* united in horror, in blood and in rape.

> Here is what I know:
> Even the most golden
> golden apple sometimes
> rolls down the long wand limb
> and lands in the lap of fire[23]

As Helen says in *The Queen of Wands*.

The fragmentation of the fabric of our myth, the myth connecting us all in a House of Women, a House of Muses, causes pain, anger, and the adoption, among Lesbians, of the role of the outcast. Audre Lorde has called her book of political essays "Sister Outsider"; Olga Broumas defines her place among women in one phrase as "kissing against the light." And in all of our work it is clear we understand our role as that of the outsider. Sappho expressed the feeling: *Like the hyacinth which shepherds tread underfoot in the mountains, and on the ground the purple flower* (Greek Lyric, 133).

Yet "outsider" is only half the term for what we do and know about what we do. For in seeking wholeness, integrity, and the utter transformation of our society, we have also been busy reconnecting to the various houses from which we come. As "outsiders" to one culture, we increasingly become insiders to several others. In becoming outsiders to a society defined mostly by men, we have certainly become insiders to a society defined by women.

Writing to Break Silences

As I said earlier, most of Sappho's work disappeared along with other ancient manuscripts; we have remnants solely because others quoted her and made copies. Through 2,600 years since Sappho's life, literary people have made so much with so little. What was in the full body of her work, the "nine books"? We can only speculate and be left with blankness. The disappearance of her work was gradual (though remembered by the dramatic image of the library at Alexandria burning) and paralleled the disappearance of most ancient wisdom. Then came long ages when women's public presence was diminished or negligible, and homoeroticism forbidden.

The 1450 invention of the Gutenberg press made literature accessible, at first to mostly men and a few women of certain classes. Centuries later, public education and the economics of small-press publishing made the work of usually disenfranchised people such as Lorde, Parker, and me possible. Widespread anti-war, civil rights, feminist, and Lesbian movements, which we all participated in, assembled audiences eager for the most honest work the four of us (and many others) could produce. We wrote and read our work into the hungers developed from long centuries of enforced silence.

During the 1970s and 1980s, a cohort of women wrote contemporary poetry from an outsider position, driving words into the old silences to break them, to shock and shake and change lives. Four Lesbian feminist poets—Adrienne Rich, Audre Lorde, Pat Parker, and myself—all wrote poetry and prose that is now richly far-flung geographically yet always in danger of disappearing, even though collectively we have published at least eighty volumes. Our work at times seems to dance together.

We four knew each other, within the intimacies of poetry and its transformational movements especially, and on the same stages at readings, and also personally. Pat and I wrote from the base of our women-only households in California, houses with multiple Lesbian housemates supporting each other in mutual enterprises for social change. On the East Coast, Audre and Adrienne, during the years I knew them, were living in separate households with their lovers; however, they met frequently in Manhattan with a group of five other women, poets, writers, therapists, a historian, all Lesbians, two Black, five white, all dedicated to social change.

Despite the distance between the coasts, we four poets knew each other, and at times we were on stage with each other. Pat and I traveled together doing readings, visited each other frequently, and I was editor and publisher for some of her books. On separate occasions, we each stayed with Audre and her lover Frances Clayton on Staten Island; Audre stayed over talking all night to Pat on the couch of a collective house, Terrace Street, in Oakland where I lived, and other times she stayed a day or two at the home I shared with Wendy Cadden, my lover in the 1970s; later, Audre stayed over at a home I shared with my lover, Paula Gunn Allen. Audre visited Parker at the home she shared with her lover Marty Dunham in Pleasant Hill, California, as did I. Wendy and I visited Adrienne one of the many times she was in the hospital recovering from operations for her rheumatoid arthritis. We also spent an afternoon in the carriage house she shared with Michele Cliff; and after they moved to the West Coast they came over for lunch one day. We did not all know each other as intimate friends, more as loving comrades intertwined because our poetry was entangled with our movement for social change and our poems were talking to each other.

We wrote intensely out of our own lives. It's one thing to write poetry complaining of one's treatment by others. It's something else to acknowledge one's own bad actions. Likewise when a poet is vested in building community interests, extolling the vulnerable community is one thing, and calling out some of its faults is a whole different level of critique.

For the contemporary poets with whom I was intertwined in the seventies and some of the eighties, critique of our culture and treatment of ourselves and others at the hands of authorities was a very real part of our content. Not for nothing is Rich's first book of the seventies named *Diving into the* **Wreck** (emphasis mine), or her concept of Lesbian and feminist movements being of necessity "disloyal to civilization." In 1967, when she was twenty-three, Parker wrote an autobiographical coming-of-age portrait of her life. Called "Goat Child," a reference to herself as a Capricorn with an indomitable stubborn will and joyful rush to live fully, the poem included a feminist critique of her ex-husband and of her society in intimate examples of sexism ("let me show you the ways of woman" / and I learned / to cook / to fuck / to wash / to fuck / to iron / to fuck")—and racism (not being served in New Mexico), but she included also details unflattering to herself, that she was clumsy, that she could not dance. The exhilarating poem ends, "the goat-child died/and a woman was born."[24]

Parker and I met in 1970 and began to read together as activist poets; we already had audiences but now we focused on rousing to solidarity and action the Gay Women's Liberation movement that my lover Wendy Cadden and I had co-founded in 1969. Parker's stunningly direct poetic was inspiring, and in 1973 I took on an autobiographical voice short on metaphor for my long poem "A Woman Is Talking to Death," like Pat letting the rhythms frame the poetic to hold the true stories. The poem weaves between oppressions, addressing, as the title suggests, social deaths I witnessed, experienced, and also participated in. The poem especially examines when I fell short in my own expectations of being a good warrior on behalf of justice for all. The poem both asks and partially answers the question: how do we, as Lesbians for instance, take love for others into the difficult world, a world of social death, of people splintered into categories of difference, locked in struggle, tearing apart. And silenced.

The poem exposes my racism as the narrator, in two different ways. The first is in the narrative of my witnessing a horrendous accident involving a Black driver and "six big policemen, all white." My lover Wendy and I had stopped, saw that the motorcyclist the driver had struck was dead, and talked to the extremely upset driver, who begged us not to leave him. But after taking his phone number, we drove off—we had an expired driver's license and were afraid for ourselves. I called his wife days later, and she did not yet know what had happened to him.

I then saw our leaving him as an abandonment, out of ignorance, a leaving, the poem says, of "all our lovers / much too soon to get the real loving done." How to do "real loving" in the face of human conflict is the subject of this complicated poem, beginning with the fact we can seldom do *enough*. The second instance of the narrator's racism is a racial slur surfacing in a fantasy of murderous revenge after having been beat up, "the simple association of one thing and another / so damned simple / my face healed / his didn't." Multiple other scenes of mistreatment: of me as a Lesbian, of me as a worker, of soldiers by their officers, of an experimental cancer patient, of an over-burdened mother, of an over-protected daughter, of a rape victim—all merge and twine in this very contemporary long poem addressing love's nemesis social "death" with a passionate dedication not to let it prevail.

What is desire for? "A Woman Is Talking to Death" plays with the idea that others are "all our lovers." "I wanted her," I wrote about a particularly injured woman, "I wanted her as a very few people have wanted / me. I wanted her and me to own and control and run the / city we lived in." I aimed the poem at state, patriarchal, and personal culpability, and also at my own white woman's ignorance, falling short in my own antiracism. I aimed the poem at the leftist-Marxist idea that homosexuality is a "decadence," and side-effect of capitalism. This complexly political poem influenced the other poets, as theirs also influenced me. Adrienne wrote later, "There are poems which . . . change the ways that it is possible for us to see and act. 'A Woman Is Talking to Death' . . . has been such a poem for me" ("Power and Danger," *The Work of a Common Woman*, 12).

Audre taught the poem in her college classes, Parker and our friend the writer Willyce Kim helped me read it on stage, and Pat used some of its imagery in "Womanslaughter," a powerful account of her sister's femicide at the hands of an ex-husband.

The year I wrote "A Woman Is Talking to Death," 1973, I think in February, Pat and I were in a writing group together, and later that summer I designed, edited, and printed, with some of the other Women's Press Collective members (notably Wendy Cadden, who illustrated it), Parker's second book with us, Pit Stop. Included was a poem that brought to the surface some contradictions between her multiple communities:

My lover is a woman
   & when i hold her -
      feel her warmth -
         i feel good - feel safe

then/I never think
   of my families' voices -
   never hear my sisters say
   bulldaggers, queers, funny,
   come see us but don't
   bring your friends

The poem builds: "My lover's hair is blonde / . . . feels like a thousand fingers / touch my skin and hold me" and "then / i . . ."

never think of Black bodies
hanging in trees or filled
with bullet holes
never hear my sisters say
white folks hair stinks
don't trust any of them

The poem continues to layer the contradictions, the safety she feels in her white lover's loving arms, juxtaposed with the white supremacist experimental cruelty of "syphilitic Black men / as guinea pigs" or genocide of "sterilized children," and the natural response of her Black sisters wanting revenge: "watch them just stop in / an intersection to *scare the old / white bitch*." Other layers bring in prejudices within the white Lesbian bar; the poet says, "her people turn and stare," asking themselves, "what defect drove her to me." The poetry doesn't spare the prejudices of Pat's own parents, her father "turning in his grave," her mother who in the poet's imagination judges Pat's Lesbianism as a bad thing, cries in repeated refrain, "Lord, what kind of child is this" (*Complete Works*, 106–7).

Caught in the middle of intersecting forces, the poet calls out all her communities as unsafe for one or another of her selves. Pat repeats this theme in another poem, "i have a dream," of wanting a revolution that could create a world in which she could bring all her selves, could hold hands openly with a lover, not be taunted by white bikers, or beaten by Black brothers, or arrested coming out of a bar: "now you listen!" the poet cries, "i have a dream too / it's a simple dream" (*Complete Works*, 90–91).

Audre was adamant that acknowledging and respecting difference meant power for the feminist movement, and that difference should be celebrated. But she did not mean that anyone should roll over for white supremacy's viciousness. A genius of metaphor and sensuality blended with hard facts, yet who had great admiration for Parker's honest, direct, inescapable drumbeat approach to social critique, Audre wrote about her own sheer rage in the face of racism. In her 1982 collection, *Chosen Poems, Old and*

Next, in "A Poem for Women in Rage," she carefully sets a dramatic scene, "like a promise I await / the woman I love" on a street corner in NY so they can go home together after work. Across the street a woman's "white face dangles / a tapestry of disasters seen / through a veneer of order":

> her mouth drawn like an ill-used roadmap
> to eyes without core, a bottled heart
> impeccable credentials of old pain.
> The veneer cracks open
> hate launches through the gaze into my afternoon
> our eyes touch like hot wire
> and the street snaps into nightmare
> a woman with white eyes is clutching
> a bottle of Fleischmann's gin
> is fumbling at her waistband
> is pulling a butcher knife from her ragged pants
> her hand arcs backward "You Black Bitch!"
> the heavy blade spins out toward me
> slow motion
> years of fury surge upward like a wall
> I do not hear it
> clatter to the pavement at my feet

The poet reacts instantly to the knife that has landed at her feet, in "hunger for resolution / simple as anger and so close at hand / my fingers reach for the familiar blade." Fortunately, in this dangerous situation her action is interrupted by the arrival of her white lover, crying out the warning, "don't touch it!"

In the remainder of the poem Audre works with conflicted feelings—the memory of the moment, "my lover's voice moves me / to a shadowy clearing" and having to make the choice between pain and rage. Another image is of a derailed train imprinted with the face of "every white woman I love / and distrust." She has recurrent dreams of the knife and revenge juxtaposed with the white lover's sleeping face next to her, "a knife at her throat." The attacker, "the woman with white eyes," has long since "vanished to become her own nightmare." But meanwhile, the poet completes her thought: "a French butcher blade hangs in my house / love's token" (Chosen Poems, 343). The narrator lets the violence of the specific event go, yet the blade remains, its potential for both vengeance and self-protection retained.

All of the poems I've discussed here acknowledge the intersectional positioning of Lesbian lives amid social splits and their violences, tempered by our responsibilities to be honest, to love and to care. In all three examples the protagonist calls out oppressive situations yet is in a place of both participant and witness, not sheer innocence or even victim—is rather in a place of vulnerable experience riding internal stormy emotions while trying to balance self-protection with moral values and a determination to forge a better world. That world is one of "all our lovers," as I called everyone in trouble in "A Woman Is Talking to Death."

Adrienne Rich added "anti-Semitism" to her list of culpabilities; born to an Episcopalian southern mother and a nonpracticing Jewish father, in 1960 she wrote:

Split at the root, neither Gentile nor Jew
Yankee nor Rebel, born
in the face of two ancient cults
I'm a good reader of histories.[25]

By 1982, in an essay she was more explicit, with "I have to face the sources and the flickering presence of my own ambivalence as a Jew; the daily, mundane anti-Semitisms of my entire life."[26] Rich's multiple social placements as outsider/insider gave her the idea of one's *moveable social locations* being more important than "identity" and a better way to move into greater accountability. And that motion-filled geographical location, she said, begins with the words "my body."[27] "Sometimes I feel I have seen too long from too many disconnected angles: white, Jewish, anti-Semite, racist, anti-racist, once-married, lesbian, middle-class, feminist, exmatriate southerner—split at the root—that I will never bring them whole."[28] She continued, "Yet we can't wait for the undamaged to shape our connections for us; we can't wait to speak until we are perfectly clear and righteous."[29]

Although we knew and visited each other, and Pat and I talked about poetry some, I don't recall that the other two discussed poetry with me very much. We shared it; Audre took my *Edward the Dyke and Other Poems* home to New York. She read Pat's early work posted on her refrigerator and commented on it. I remember Audre bringing her newly published *The Black Unicorn* to a visit with me, and how proud she was of it. I carried that book with me for inspiration everywhere the first year I worked on *The Queen of Wands*.

While we didn't intently talk about our work to each other, our poems with their intersectional messages do seem to be talking to each other, through the hearts' psyche that reduces distance and, for precious moments, appreciates differences. Intersectional, yes, offering race, class, sexual orientation, maternity, and other categories that have now solidified into social hierarchies. The dynamics within the poems also could be called *transectional*, a term I have drawn from the geological science of studying cross sections of rock levels, the strata reflecting when and how the layers formed: here is a carbonaceous band from ancient life, then a bed of silica-rich chert, here is the coarse granite layer, next the intrusive metamorphic igneous, here is the well-baked beautiful marble, and so on. While the layers of rock in a cut or upheaved mountain seem fixed, they are each product of ferocious heated movement under pressure, fiery extrusions from the burning core, sudden melting flows, impact of ice and rain and ever-changing life forms. And the mantle itself is both solid and molten, always transforming.

Transectional can also be used as a verb, *transecting*, an ongoing or periodical process of making one's own moral inventory, continuing to examine the layers that make up a life—what did I show up for, what did I neglect, where was I cruel and self-righteous, who is trying to hurt me? What do I not yet know? What did I forget? We are in changing times, and times in need of our changes being conscious, directed by ourselves. How do our layers become fixed? How does change happen? How, transecting asks, *how* do we change? How do we use the wisdoms gained from our own changes to help others change? We are seldom if ever "already knowing." We are learning creatures, we study and adjust. We make mistakes, experience shame, try again. We do our best, then say that isn't good enough. We project our failures onto others, in part because as poets have said, seeing ourselves is not easy, yet it is necessary to try, and to mirror this process for our cultures.

Transecting helps us see ourselves with honesty and track our progress toward comprehending when we are wrong and fulfilling our beliefs about ourselves as "good." Perhaps "good" isn't even a good goal. What about Adrienne saying of herself and Audre, "the terrible mothers we both dread and long to be." Pat emphatically stated, in the closing lines of *Womanslaughter*, her poem about her sister's murder:

I have gained many sisters
and if one is beaten,
or raped, or killed
I will not come in mourning black
I will not pick the right flowers
I will not celebrate her death
& it will matter not
if she's Black or white —
if she loves women or men
I will come with my many sisters
and decorate the streets
with the innards of those
brothers in womanslaughter (*Complete Works*, 156).

Audre said, in the voice of an Amazon warrior of Dahomey, she is "warming whatever I touch / that is living / consuming / only / what is already dead" (*Collected Poems*, 242), devouring and casting away the parts of the culture that are rotten, and oppressive. Then coming in with new ideas. My own "A Woman Is Talking to Death" ends with the poet swearing absolute dedication to leading a just life with "nothing left of me for you / ho death," meaning, of course, social death. Social death is held in place through small and large hatreds, punishments, neglect, and silences. This is the "civilization" to which Adrienne was disloyal, the same set of restrictions to which I declared, "I'm not a girl / I'm a hatchet." And Pat announced, "I, Woman, must be / the child of myself."

Transectional applied to poetic exploration uncovers layers of selves unpeeling to reveal themselves like the bands of differently textured, layered stone in a slice of mountain: here is the loving self, here is the suffering one, here is the self-righteous but not very good one, here is the murderous vengeful one, here is the generously just one.

Parker wrote of having a "simple dream" of a revolution enabling her to bring all her selves with her wherever she goes: female, Black, Lesbian, united with white as well as Black, Indigenous, and people of color, as lovers. Audre used the term "shattered selves," Adrienne, "split at the root." I too, have selves in contradictory positions, seeking to knit them together with my works out of my life experiences, which advocate for LGBTQ peoples, for cultural feminism, for woman-centered spirituality, for neurodivergence, for radical critique of white supremacy, for consciousness within all creatures, for new origin stories that are inclusive at their very base.

Audre said, "The failure of academic feminists to recognize difference as crucial strength is a failure to reach beyond the first patriarchal lesson in our world; divide and conquer must become define and empower" ("The Master's Tools Will Never Dismantle the Master's House," *This Bridge Called My Back*, 98-101). We experienced both our layers of self and our relation to different groups as shattered because our cultures have shattered apart different groups, as well as experiences of self. There is a correlation here. The poetry of all four of us shows how we struggled to, as Audre put it, "make our shattered faces whole," and in that process we became ever more expansive, and ever more precise, exploring not only oppressions but also women's history, mythology, and contributions to the human adventure.

Because women's bodies are so objectified in US mainstream culture, one aspect of our chosen task of reclamation of ourselves as women, and women as persons, was some rewriting of women's bodies. In particular, breasts were addressed by all four of us, to surprising effects.

Did Sappho write about her lovers' breasts? Not simply their clothing? Did she describe their bodies? Would such descriptions have been delicate and beautiful, "a fern unfolding," as Rich said? Fulsome and maternal as were the older goddesses who displayed their breasts of abundance and generosity? Daringly erotic, as I wrote for a lover in 1967:

in the place where
her breasts come together
two thumbs' width of
channel ride my
eyes to anchor
hands to angle
in the place where
her legs come together
I said 'you smell like the
ocean' and lay down my tongue
beside the dark tooth edge
of sleeping
'swim' she told me and I
did, I did.[30]

By 1972 I had taken on breasts as protective power in a She Who poem: "I shall grow another breast / in the middle of my chest / what shall it be / . . . I'm going to groom her with my tongue / . . . She Who defends me" (love belongs, 76).

For a woman to write about breasts—or indeed sex, physical desire, in the 1960s and 1970s was fractious, daring, with a labyrinth of possible drastic findings, spurred by the absence of the socially maternal, the ecologically maternal, the psycho-spiritually maternal, in our entire mainstream culture. We needed new imagery, new language, as Rich wrote, "good enough for our descriptions of the world we are trying to transform" ("Power and Danger," The Work of a Common Woman, 21). As feminists, of course the four of us wanted to avoid cliches of our own or other women's bodies as commodities or objects; we wanted to describe power, vulnerability, and connection.

In "A Woman Dead in Her Forties," Rich described a small group of women friends sitting in the sun with blouses off, unashamed, except for one who pulls her blouse back on in hasty embarrassment, and the poet wrote:

I barely look at you
as if my look could scald you
though I'm the one who loved you

I wanted to touch my fingers
to where your breasts had been
but we never did such things[31]

Lines both tender and fiery that simply dissolve me. Lines written in the age of rampaging cancer, especially breast cancer, and its great public silences, which women poets among others helped to break open.

In 1974 Audre returned from a trip to Africa having been profoundly moved by a rotting wooden ikon of Yoruba mother goddess Seboulisa, about which she wrote, in "Dahomey":

It was in Abomey that I felt
the full blood of my fathers' wars
and where I found my mother
Seboulisa
standing with outstretched palms hip high
one breast eaten away by worms of sorrow.
(Collected Poems, 239)

In 1979 Audre had her breast cancer diagnosis and began her journey of survival through what she would call, with righteous bitterness, "the cancer industry." Within a short time she had a mastectomy, refusing afterwards to wear a prosthesis to look "normal," instead sporting a heavy protective African necklace on the breastless side of her chest. Proudly refusing to bow to body conformity and cover-up of loss, she wrote about her experiences and opinions of the medical system in The Cancer Journals.

Then after a few years Pat was also diagnosed with cancer and had a mastectomy. In letters, the two more than reconciled their differences and sensitivities, as they fell into a profound sisterlove expressed in letters and phone calls until Pat's death in 1989. Responding to Pat's mastectomy, Audre wrote, "Think of yourself as a one-breasted dahomeian amazon. It helps counter balance the sense of loss. I'm glad you're getting into your body. She's different, and she's yours. Love her" (*Sister Love*, 91). In "To Audre," Pat wrote:

After I read *The Cancer Journals*
I made love to you

touched your body – pressed
my hands deep into your flesh
and passed my warmth to you.
I kissed the space where
your right breast had been
ran my tongue over your body
      to lick away your fear
      to lick away my fear.
(*Complete Works*, 180)

To use both Black and Lesbian love for healing is not uncommon; to use it on a powerful psychic plane, and then put that into a poem for all to read—that is amazing.

Most people fall all over Audre for her poetry, Pat wrote in a letter to her, and "I study it" but "I feel closer to you through your prose. There's a vulnerability there that makes me want to gather you into my arms" (*Sister Love*, 86). In preparation to describe her medical condition at length, Pat wrote apologetically, "hearing this must be somewhat like being in a relationship with someone younger than yourself—retracing a lot of familiar ground" (78). Audre replied emphatically, "Listen, love, it's not like being in a relationship with someone younger than myself—although you are. It's like being in a relationship with a beloved part of my own self" (88).

The theme of women really looking at unspoken realities of our lives surfaced for me in my verse play *The Queen of Swords*, written during a time of intense grappling with chronic inner turmoil and physical illness, residue of an abused childhood. Set in a Lesbian bar where an aloof disembodied Helen of Troy character full of denial is shocked when the Amazon warrior Penthesilea, who died for her in the battle at Troy, and whose body has partially rotted away, rises up from the floor and confronts her. The ghostly warrior challenges contemporary Helen:

Though you recoil from me now
dressed in my blood and dirt,
and with my wounded breast—
is my sack of being
too leaky for your good taste?
(*Judy Grahn Reader*, 171)

Penthesilea concludes, "oh I know I offend you / with my . . . / . . . bitter words . . . my messages of hard reality. But Helen . . . reach to touch me, tangle fingers with me now / so you can remember who you are / and I can live on earth again." Helen, tremulously, reaches out, touches her, recoils, ends with, "Now another woman's blood is on my hands" (174).

Each poet came to a place of love and desired connection in the midst of physical and emotional chaos. We used other kinds of images for breasts, of course. Audre was especially diverse, for instance merging human body with the land: "curvatures of sand / nipples of sand / hard erected bosoms of sand;"[72] and invitationally: "under the breasts of a summer night" (277); and sumptuously: "I dream of a place between your breasts / to build my house like a haven / where I plant crops / in your body / an endless harvest" (297). Audre, who listed her identities, or selves, as badges of honor: "Black, mother, lesbian, warrior, poet," wrote often of children, Black boys murdered by police for instance, and her own urge to give maternal comfort to abused children: "Winter has come and the children are dying. / / One begs me to hold her between my breasts" (247). Most powerfully, in "The Women of Dan Dance with Swords in Their Hands to Mark the Time When They Were Warriors," Audre wrote:

I do not come like a secret warrior
with an unsheathed sword in my mouth
hidden behind my tongue
slicing my tongue to ribbons
of service with a smile
while the blood runs
down and out
through holes in the two sacred mounds
in my chest

(242)

Returning to the subject of desire, and the question of what is really wanted, my poem "Talkers in a Dream Doorway" was written for Adrienne, following an intense (for me) small dinner party of seven writers in Manhattan. Audre pulled me onto her lap; Adrienne danced with me. I was already in thrall with them because I had just written The Highest Apple, first edition, and the love inherent in their poems had passed into me. I was bursting. And later wrote about the dance as a moment of desire—for what? Not simply to flirt, to teasingly kiss, something deeper, a desire for power, personal and social:

> . . . unity
> such as we thought could render up the constellations
> AND our
> daily lives, justice, equality AND freedom,
> give us worldly definition
> AND the bread of belonging. In my imagination
> I see my fingers curled round the back of your head
> as though your head were your breast
> and I were pulling it to me.
> As though your head were your breast
> and I were pulling it to me.
>
> I admit I have wanted to possess your mind.
> (love belongs, 255)

The poem continues with its theme of underlying desires: "I admit I have wanted to possess my own life" and for a world of women, "we want to / suck a new language, strike a thought into being, out of the old / fleshpot. That rotten old body of our long submersion"—a dream of woman-to-woman bonded desire extended into social transformation.

Did Sappho write anything like these lines during her times of exile, or any other times? Do such sentiments live like ghosts in the work of hers that is lost to us? Sappho's voice in some of her poems reflects values of speaking with self-revealing honesty; when she talks about the pain of her own envy, or begs Aphrodite to turn someone's heart to her. What other self-revelations she might have written, we don't know, unless more fragments of her lost volumes should surface.

Or was she really mostly interested in elegant clothing, well-woven sandals, flowers in soft hair? Perhaps Sappho too, like Adrienne, and the rest of us, was writing from a geography of her body. And she also had given the ancient template for aesthetics with her answer to what is "the most beautiful thing on the black earth," as *whatsoever one loves*.

An Ideal Place of Wholeness Appears in All Our Work

An ideal place appears in much of the imagery of Lesbian poets: in a similar way that Rich has used Stonehenge, H.D. used the white island and the sacred orchard; Lowell used the garden and Dickinson used her own unique concept of "heaven"—not the patriarchal heaven, but the one where she would find her own name and could reunite with her lost female love. In a similar way, many Lesbians have thought of Lesbos as an ideal place, home, where one is central to one's own life, and where the women are bonding, are sisters—and more than sisters. Where there is a House of Women, a myth, a place of centrality.

In each poet this ideal place of wholeness is expressed differently.[33] This place of home base is alternately longed for and defined by Lorde. It is a name she seeks to learn, a "tree under which she is lying," the lover's (that is, Woman's) body she would like to plant crops of the future on ("October," *Chosen Poems*, 108–9).

In Allen's poetry this place is called "home" and home is idea—"an idea of ourselves is what we own."[34] In my work the place itself is found in each other, gained through "work"—by which I mean the interactions, the yeast of creative effort, as "to work magic"—as well as decision, resolve. With Adrienne Rich, the home place is mind, and choice. From "Twenty-One Love Poems":

XV

If I lay on that beach with you
white, empty, pure green water warmed by the Gulf Stream
and lying on that beach we could not stay
because the wind drove fine sand against us
as if it were against us
if we tried to withstand it and we failed—
if we drove to another place
to sleep in each other's arms
and the beds were narrow like prisoners' cots
and we were tired and did not sleep together
and this was what we found, so this is what we did—
was the failure ours?
If I cling to circumstances I could feel
not responsible. Only she who says
she did not choose, is the loser in the end.
(*Dream of a Common Language*, 32–33)

As I said earlier, in "Twenty-One Love Poems," Rich locates a new place, a not-Stonehenge-simply, but the mind "casting back" to a shared solitude "chosen without loneliness." This place equals an end to the alienation that has been the price of forming any little piece of a House of Women bonded—when it has been secretive, as "two against the world." Rich walks into this new place, a place of both "heavy shadows and great light." "I choose to be a figure in that light," she says, "I choose to walk here. And to draw this circle" (36).

Building communities that can center in a House of Women has figured strongly in our work and in our lives also, since we believe our work, and act on it. Building communities means making cross-connections and healing the torn places in the social fabric of myth we have each inherited, but that the outcast especially inherits. No trace of this ripped fabric of fragmented life is evident in Sappho's work, besides that the work is itself in fragments, and she herself has been shredded so often. But anti-Lesbianism and institutionalized misogyny developed centuries after she wrote as a highly esteemed citizen in what must have been a remarkably intact holistic society.

Paula Gunn Allen writes of the creatrix, the primary god (Spider Grandmother) of the Keres Pueblo people:

> she was given the work of weaving the strands
> of her body, her pain, her vision,
> into creation, and the gift of having created,
> to disappear
> . . . After her I sit on my laddered rain-bearing rug
> and mend the tear with string.[35]

After Sappho, the others of us who are doing this work sit mending tears in the fabrics of our myth also, mending the tears in the tales Sappho said Love weaves, mending the tapestries the old women storytellers once made of the substance of a wholistic life, its spider meanings.

We are mending the rips and tears, yes. And we are doing more. We are attempting, I believe, what Stein accomplished when she broke the culture trance between the objective and subjective worlds. We are, each in our own unique way, attempting to completely rearrange a particular way of thinking, to turn it inside out. We are taking on the forces within us and outside us, as Rich says:

> this we were, and this is how we tried to love,
> and these are the forces they had ranged against us,
> and these are the forces we had ranged within us,
> within us and against us, against us and within us.
> (*Dream of a Common Language*, 34)

Rich writes into a women's version of history and into a sense of the intellect that includes mystic elements to make her demanding critiques of modern civilization. She holds womanly qualities up as a model for behavior: let the men have the courage of women, she says, and meanwhile in her lover's small, strong hands she can trust the world.

For each of us, the points of contact differ, the Houses of Women have different origins and are woven of slightly different stuff. Broumas, for instance, waded into the common Western European myths of women. Simply by completely restructuring Leda and the Swan, eliminating the former rapist/Zeus/father, she rearranged the relation of the female to what impregnates her. The Swan, she said, was another woman. In this outrageous act, she opened the world of Western mythology, so it became easy, even less radical, for me to walk into the myth of

Helen in *The Queen of Wands* and interpret it according to my own intuitions, history, and research.

I think that it is my ability to place the exotic, extreme, and overlooked stereotypes of the woman—not only of common women, but of queens and whores, wives and dykes—into a place of tradition and centrality that gives my work its "re-membering" qualities. It restructures the usual patriarchal myth of feminine/masculine class structure. In my work the most hidden, taboo qualities of a woman's life are pulled to the surface and seen not only as charged and magical, but as having integrated mythical reality—as reaching back and forth in time—as defining qualities central to all woman-centered power.

Audre Lorde in the special mediumship of her work takes full force the racial as well as sexual stereotyping for the stuff of her exploration of the inside and the outside. The feared "other," she says in dozens of ways, is a projection of ourselves: "I think you / afraid I was mama as laser / seeking to eat out or change your substance" she wrote in "Letter for Jan" (*The Black Unicorn*, 88). She speaks of "all her faces." And in "Dream/Songs from the Moon in Beulah Land," she specifies the special projection of stereotyping: "If I were drum / you would beat me / listening for the echo / of your own touch" (75). And the functions of the woman warrior in our society she defines succinctly and brilliantly:

I come like a woman
who I am
spreading out through nights
laughter and promise
and dark heat

warming whatever I touch
that is living
consuming
only
what is already dead.

(14)

Paula Gunn Allen's work also seeks to unhook a culture trance that has racial definitions as a major basis for its terrible operations. In many of her poems, Allen juxtaposes the material world and the spiritual world, tugging and tugging at the Western definitions of what is alive, what is dead, what has meaning.

All of this is a conscious effort to alter and break the "culture trance" of the belief system around us, so we can speak our own truths, from the basis of our own lives. We speak them out into a world at large, which then learns its own interpretations and makes its own uses of what we say.

Mythic Realism and a House of Women

"Mythic realism" is a phrase I have used for years to help myself understand what I am doing and what my contemporaries are doing in their art. I invented it (so far as I know), thinking about both poetry and the visual arts. For instance, Michelangelo's statue David has a realistic human body but a mythological name, from David and Goliath, the tale of a human defeating a monstrous giant. Van Gogh's Starry Night paintings, with enlarged brilliant sky orbs and their whirling auras along with energy swirls between them, convey an emotion of awe and, for me, shivers. Artemisia Gentileschi, a seventeenth-century Baroque painter, created a portrayal of the Biblical story of Judith cutting off the head of villain Holofernes in vivid realistic detail. Contemporary artist Irmajean portrayed Jesus as a Black woman crucified on a cross, seen from above the earth, which served as the cover illustration for Parker's third book, Womanslaughter. In other words, artists and writers combine realism and mythology all the time.

All of them use human subjects portrayed realistically on one level, yet with deep connections to a communally held myth at the same time. Mythic realism means to me that when myth and reality are combined, the result is art based on both our collective consciousness and collective unconsciousness. Gay writer Robert Gluck, heavily influenced by Lesbian/feminism as well as his own Jewish and Gay cultures, speaks of taking into account both the local (the community and the individual) and the sublime (the unknown and unknowable). The village and the wilderness, as Paula Gunn Allen might say. In contrast, Pat Parker does not use myth or even metaphor in the same way, though in heightening, intensifying the dramas she witnessed and experienced, she rhythmically and emphatically mythologizes her own life and her values.

"Mythic realism" describes much of the work of the contemporary Lesbian poets discussed here. Audre Lorde called Zami a "biomythography" from the same perspective.[36] Zami is partly a biography, based in physical fact, and partly it is mythic, drawing strong erotic/power essence from the great stream (the cultural dream stream) of African/Caribbean/Black American Orisha (gods). In Zami this myth is carried in the person of the ever-intriguing lover character Kitty, who is really the old woman poet-warrior-god Afrikete manifested in the flesh in the Gay culture of Harlem.

We do not take the sacred, the political, the social, the details of the everyday, and carry them "away" or split them from each other. We place them all together in the real lives of real women in the present, in the raucous, dangerous, tumultuous marketplace/urban/warzone/ suburb of modern life. As Sappho did. In this way we help to re-found Houses of Women from which to approach all other worlds, re-connections to the Roses of the Muses, making more intact the fabric of Lesbian myth.

III:
TO SURFACE WiTH LESBIAN GODS

And Sappho said this:

Hesperus, (evening star) bringing everything that shining Dawn scattered, you bring the sheep, you bring the goat, you bring back the child to its mother.[1]

Many gods lived in Sappho's world, and her fragments have considerable reference to them. Although her favorite was Aphrodite, also called Cyprus, the Cyprian, after her island of origin, Sappho also speaks of Hermes the cup bearer, of Adonis, Hymen, Hera, Zeus, Ares, Hephaistos, the "holy, rosy-armed" Graces and the Muses.

In some poems she is calling the gods to her: *Hither again, Muses, leaving the golden (house of your Father, Zeus)* and *Hither now, tender Graces and lovely-haired Muses* (131). Quite directly and simply, "come here." In others, she is describing their behavior: *There a bowl of ambrosia had been mixed and Hermes took the jug and poured wine for the gods* (155). Or praising their being, as in *Let your (graceful form appear) near me (while I pray) lady Hera* (69).

Beauty, love, grace filled her descriptions of the gods, even in their persons: *It is not easy for us to rival the goddesses in loveliness of figure*, she sang (123). And in another song, *but I love delicacy . . . love has obtained for me the brightness and beauty of the sun* (101). Not physical appearance of love and beauty alone does she praise, however, for appropriate behavior also plays a part in her aesthetic teachings: *for he that is beautiful is fair as appearances go, while he that is good will consequently also be beautiful* (97).

Many of her fragments appear to be instruction in appropriate behavior and attitudes to bear toward the gods. When she says it is not right that there should be lamentation in the house of those who serve the Muses, the reason given is, *That would not be fitting for us* (161). In another poem, the speaker asks Aphrodite (here called Cytherea): *Delicate Adonis is dying, Cytherea; what are we to do?* and the goddess answers with explicit instructions: *Beat your breasts, girls, and tear your clothes* (155).

The appropriate behavior centered often (or at least the fragments indicate this) on the proper dress for pleasing the gods:

> *and you, Dica, put lovely garlands around your locks, binding together stems of anise with your soft hands; for the blessed Graces look rather on what is adorned with flowers and turn away from the ungar- landed.* (109)

It is monumentally purposeful, then, this wearing of flowers that appears so often in her words; flowers will draw the attention of the gods and spirits, and they will favor us. They are gods who love brightness and heavy odors and vivid colors; they are not gods of severity and deprivation.

In speculating on what the gods, what holiness and spirituality, meant to Sappho (and therefore could possibly mean to us, in our world, and in our traditional connection to her), I have found it useful to look at the names of flowers and colors she mentioned. In poetry that lasts, virtually nothing is accidental or without a larger-than-surface meaning. Flowers have mythic dimension because of the sacred (and otherwise) stories told of them over the centuries.

Lilies, for instance, have become Christian symbols of purity, death, and resurrection. The daisy is a homey, trustworthy flower in song and poem representing the loyal love of a good-hearted woman. Neither of these occurs in Sappho's fragments. Her flowers are the rose, violet, hyacinth, golden chick-pea, lotus, anise, and chervil. The rose, of course, recurs throughout Western literature as the supreme natural manifestation of the bio-essentially female. Along with the apple, or similar red fruit such as pomegranate, the rose conjures the vulva with its birthing, sexual/creative, and menstrual/intuitive powers. The red rose signifies power, eroticism, and creativity on the deepest levels.

Perhaps, in fact, when Sappho speaks of the reddening sweet-apple at the topmost bough, the one that the apple pickers could not reach—she is singing a song of special protection over the essential womanly powers: they will never, quite, be reached, and taken from us.

Gold is a color often repeated in Sappho's lines, especially with relation to Aphrodite, god of love, who is described as golden-throned, as golden-crowned, as coming from a golden house, as pouring nectar into golden cups. This seems appropriate for the poet of love, since gold is the traditional color associated with love, as modern wedding ring customs testify. I personally believe that gold is a color seen in a love-induced psychic state. Sappho reported seeing a color that was *more golden than gold*; Aphrodite's head (aura?) she saw as *golden-crowned*, and love was gold-colored to her for she said that *love has obtained for me the brightness and beauty of the sun* (101).

A color almost as prominent as gold in Sappho's work is purple. In the sparse fragments left of her work there are fourteen references to purple or to violets and other purple flowers. In my book *Another Mother Tongue: Gay Words, Gay Worlds*, I devote an entire chapter to the many stories connecting the color purple to Gay themes and stories of same-sex lovers of different genders.[2] The chapter cites other themes describing purple as the color of Gay shamanic/priesthoods of ancient tribes. It is the most highly spiritual color of the sacred and occult world itself, often a Gay province in human cultures that have not suppressed it. Purple, lavender, the amethyst and amaranth, the violet, the pansy, and the hyacinth all figure in Gay stories. Not surprisingly, these purple references are also associated with Gay gods—Artemis the hunter, for instance, Apollo and his lover Hyacinthus, and others. This gives me a special way to identify with Sappho's poignant description *Like the hyacinth which shepherds tread underfoot and on the ground the purple flower* (Greek Lyric, 133).

That she bonded with women, then, and worshipped forces described with homosexual (as well as heterosexual) themes, that her lavender-flowered island itself was a center for the sacredness of women's bonding, are important to understanding her tradition, and ours. Her gods are part of her intact culture. She called them to her in person, and she addressed them in sleep: *I spoke to you in a dream*, she says of Aphrodite. She welcomes Aphrodite to come to her own special orchard, where cold water babbles through apple branches, the altar is smoking with incense, and the whole place is shadowed in roses. How powerfully feminine a place this is.

Artemis, Sappho says, lives unwed in the wild mountains, and Love, loosener of limbs, never comes near her. Now men and gods alike call her the virgin, shooter of deer, hunter (91).

In a culture whose prime product was fine wine, Sappho's gods pour from golden cups and jugs golden libations, nectars, and wines for each other with great frequency. There is no fear of death, in Sappho's mind. The land beyond death is flower-covered, too. She sometimes craves it; she says, *I get no pleasure from being above the earth, and a longing grips me to die and see the dewy, lotus-covered banks of Acheron* (119). This death is not oblivion, nor is it the same as the Christian heaven. It is more like the spirit world described in some tribal traditions, a dream that exists next to this one, through which the gods and spirits pass back and forth with messages and mysteries. Immortality was assured to Sappho because her dream is a true one. *Someone, I say, will remember us in the future,* she is confident (159). The only death is detachment from the dream, from the myth, from the House of the Muses. The woman who does that, Sappho says, who has no share in their roses, will wander all through her poor death among corpses, unseen, *flown from our midst,* and no one will remember her or long for her at all (99). That is death, the only possible one. All else is a continuation of expressive, passionate, lovely and loving life.

Far and away the major theme of Sappho's work is Love, love as manifested in the form of the great Aphrodite or as her servant, Eros. Love, Sappho says, is a taleweaver, and also bitter-sweet, a snare, a "limb-loosener." Sappho's Love god is sexual and aesthetic, sacred and profane, profound and trivial. Persuasion aids Aphrodite in gaining love for the mortals, and clearly trickery also figures in. I am going to assume that Sappho's Aphrodite was a goddess of intelligence, aesthetic balance, and vision as well as of beauty and love. I believe this because there is no reason not to; her world was not severely fragmented, as ours has become.

There is no indication of the terrible division we have been taught to make between the physical and the spiritual, between the body and the mind, between the sexual and the sacred, between beauty and the beast. Consider for a moment the role of dimwit that the greatest symbol of Love and Beauty of our culture, Marilyn Monroe, was forced to play—in spite of her desperate desire to be respected for her acting, for her intellect, for her desire to write poetry. She was portrayed as a dumb, empty-headed shell of a person, for the benefit of the men who said this was the entirety of their idea of "beauty."

When the apple of woman-bonding has shriveled and is hidden from sight, when the island of women's centrality is out of reach, has sunk like Atlantis, and when the Houses of Women speaking common language are silenced, alienation is all that can follow. For women are central to society. When we are split from that centrality and integrity, all society splinters and suffers.

And now, keeping in mind the memory of Aphrodite as a complex goddess with thousands of attributes, let us leave Sappho in her nearly buried world and go on through the loss of the old gods to their possible reclamation in our modern Lesbian poetry. For in looking at our gods, at the spiritual elements and the underlying mythic dreams indigenous to our poetry, we can tell something about the integrity of the work and its relation to the movement of feminism, Lesbian feminism, and the women's culture it represents, that I believe is straining to recoup its highest apple.

The Heaven of Dickinson's Drama

Emily Dickinson worked out, in poetic form, a one-sided dialogue with—virtually an argument with—the god of her father's house, sometimes finding his love enough and other times challenging it with the strength of her own love. Her own love was primarily for women, for the natural elements, and for the "heaven" she sought. Her heaven would be the joining of women, complete in their quality of "queens," and together with each other in a world far different from the constricted one of Amherst where she lived as such an eccentric, brilliant, angry wraith.

"Heaven"—is what I cannot reach!
The Apple on the Tree—
Provided it do hopeless—hang—
That—"Heaven" is—to Me!

The Color, on the Cruising Cloud—
The interdicted Land—
Behind the Hill—the House behind—
There—Paradise—is found!

Her teasing Purples—Afternoons—
The credulous—decoy—
Enamored—of the Conjuror—
That spurned us—Yesterday![3]

The poem is possibly based on Sappho's sweet-apple reddening on the bough-top.

Interdicted means prohibited, forbidden, "The interdicted land behind the hill, the house behind; there—paradise is found," so Emily described the Lesbian place, a place of "teasing purples" where the Sapphic apple hangs (still helpless) on the tree, for "heaven is what I cannot reach!" In one poem she is explicit that the heaven she envisions is not the Christian one of her father:

Peruse how infinite I am
To no one that You—know—
And sigh for lack of Heaven—but not
The Heaven God bestow—

(315)

Heaven for Emily had a female base. Writing as a woman, she competes with Jesus over their capacities to love:

So well that I can live without—
I love thee—then How well is that?
As well as Jesus!
Prove it to me
That He—loved Men—
As I—love thee—

(219)

Perhaps it was the very impossibility of her poetry really reaching a public audience in her lifetime that enabled her, alone in her room and in her private packets of paper, to so boldly confront the god of the fathers, to challenge his claim to omnipotence. Her poetry expresses open longing for a different kind of heaven. She speaks of time, of death, and of longing for love in the same epic terms as any mystic, while living there in the house of her Calvinist father who did not believe in dreams, in art, and who had no use for poetry nor even for books.

> God is indeed a jealous God—
> He cannot bear to see
> That we had rather not with Him
> But with each other play.
>
> (698)

What the suffering of the unrequited female love we know she pined for, could buy, she indicated with this Christian imagery:

> Each was to each The Sealed Church,
> Permitted to commune this—time—
> . . .
> And so when all the time had leaked,
> Without external sound
> Each bound the Other's Crucifix—
>
> We gave no other Bond—
>
> Sufficient troth, that we shall rise—
> Deposed—at length, the Grave—
> To that new Marriage,
> Justified—through Calvaries of Love—
>
> (153)

She is literally calling for marriage beyond the grave, a new marriage and a new love—which I take to be Lesbian love—justified by the suffering for its loss. Repeatedly she looked to the future, to life beyond the grave, as a possible place to enact the marriage of two queens. That she was keenly aware of a "lost past" that needs to be restored is stunningly evident in this argument with the patriarchal god:

If "God is Love" as he admits
We think that he must be
Because he is a "jealous God"
He tells us certainly

If "All is possible with" him
As he besides concedes
He will refund us finally
Our confiscated Gods—

(552)

A rich variety of colors recur in Dickinson's metaphors drawn from the natural world of meadows, gardens, and landscapes she daily witnessed in Amherst. But no color occurs more frequently than does the classic Gay color, purple. She uses purple, violets, and the stone amethyst repeatedly in her poems. Purple is "the color of a Queen" (378), she says in one poem, and we know she used "Queen" to indicate the fulfilled woman, especially when there are two queens together.

The following is a poem that perfectly describes her experience of gaining and then losing a woman's love:

I held a Jewel in my fingers—
And went to sleep—

The day was warm, and winds were prosy—
I said, "'Twill keep"—
I woke—and chid my honest fingers
The Gem was gone—
And now, an Amethyst remembrance
Is all I own—

(112)

The poem was written about the period of time when Kate Scott wrote her a letter apparently breaking off as hopeless their intensely passionate two-year relationship. The major themes of lost love and of a possible heaven consisting of reuniting, of at last being two queens together, recurred throughout Dickinson's work, evidently constructed of the love she had for Kate Scott and, more consistently, for Sue Gilbert Dickinson.

Emily Dickinson was influenced by the teachings of the more formal Transcendentalists of her time. Their mystic and idealistic beliefs stressed the intuition of the individual rather than logic and externally imposed structures and stated that an Emersonian "Oversoul" connects us to natural life on earth and the rest of the universe. Even more, pure metaphysics shines through in this poem on the nature of mortality, the illusion that is our notion of death. She herself, as the poet, knows we live in a long deathless dream, a "Drama" as she calls it:

We dream—it is good we are dreaming—
It would hurt us—were we awake—
But since it is playing—kill us,
And we are playing—shriek—
What harm? Men die—externally—
It is a truth—of Blood—

But we—are dying in Drama—
And Drama—is never dead—

Cautious—We jar each other—
And either—opens the eyes—
Lest the Phantasm—prove the Mistake—
And the livid Surprise

Cool us to Shafts of Granite—
With just an Age—and Name—
And perhaps a phrase in Egyptian—
It is prudenter—to dream—

(259–60)

The "Drama" here is something similar to Sappho's House of the Muses—if we unhook from it, we will fall out of the myth and "cool . . . to Shafts of Granite—/ With just an Age and Name—," become simply historical and material—and finite. Drama, she says, is never dead. The poem is so complex and so ahead of her time that I had to learn about Eric Berne's "Game Theory" of psychology *and* read Jane Roberts's messages from Seth[4] to understand it.

From Drama to a "Real Dream"

To my knowledge, Amy Lowell did not preoccupy herself with the re-establishment of the lost female godhead except indirectly through descriptions of her lover that compared her to a god, or at any rate said that her shawl, "the colour of red violets— / Flares out behind you in great curves / Like the swirling draperies of a painted Madonna."[5] More amusingly, more bitingly, and more essentially erotic/sacred, she wrote this one:

Venus Transiens

Tell me,
Was Venus more beautiful
Than you are,
When she topped
The crinkled waves,
Drifting shoreward
On her plaited shell?
Was Botticelli's vision
Fairer than mine;
And were the painted rosebuds
He tossed to his lady,
Of better worth
Than the words I blow about you
To cover your too great loveliness
As with a gauze
Of misted silver?
For me,
You stand poised
In the blue and buoyant air,
Cinctured by bright winds,
Treading the sunlight.
And the waves which preceed you
Ripple and stir
The sands at my feet.
(Complete Poetical Works, 210)

Hilda Doolittle concerned herself with little else than describing the power of the female godhead, although the thin amount of attention she has received in anthologies has focused on her shortest poems. Supposed to illustrate the form of "Imagism," these poems constitute the very smallest part of what she was doing. It is her content, the unfolding epic women's content of her fully developed work, that marks her as a great poet.

In keeping with being herself a beautiful woman who spent much of her life defining the nature of love, she had complete identification with Helen, goddess of beauty, who is the equivalent, for some European-based cultures, of Aphrodite. H.D. wrote much of her work after experiencing the ravishing period of the World Wars. She and her longtime lover Bryher daringly and typically moved to London during the two-hundred-day *blitzkrieg* in order to see for themselves what was happening to their civilization. H.D. took as subject the war at Troy, the war that saw Helen fall from power as the queen and god she had been prior to that time. In "The Walls Do Not Fall," H.D. spoke out of her poetical reality of London wracked with bombing, as all civilization trembled in the West, and men came home altered from the corpse field and the giant factories of death.

In *Helen in Egypt*, H.D. relives the war of Troy, taking the unique position that Helen was not there, only a dream of Helen walked the ramparts, only an illusion, an empty sleeve, a scarf. The real Helen, she said, was in Egypt all that time, in the occult land of her origin; she was on an island having dialogues with Achilles and other figures from the war. And by removing Helen from the war, from her downfall and death, from her own loss, H.D. is saying she can still be found, and found intact. In the occult and Hermetic and other ancient traditions, Helen as a god lives still, love as intelligence lives still, and can be found.

One of the finest sources of that knowledge, H.D. says in one angry poem, is in language itself, and in the work of poets. For we are actually "bearers of the secret wisdom." She says for critics to say that "poets are useless" or "pathetic"—

> this is the new heresy;
> but if you do not even understand what words say,
>
> how can you expect to pass judgment
> on what words conceal?
>
> yet the ancient rubrics reveal that
> we are back at the beginning:
>
> you have a long way to go,
> walk carefully, speak politely
>
> to those who have done their worm-cycle,
> for gods have been smashed before
>
> and idols and their secret is stored
> in man's very speech,
>
> in the trivial or
> the real dream[6]

In the "real dream" H.D. described seeing the female god, probably in a vision. H.D. was extremely visionary, even to the point of being considered psychotically so, having had five episodes in her life for which she was sometimes hospitalized. Her description of the goddess at the end of the following seems extremely realistic to me, not at all a metaphor, or reference (as the beginning of the poem is) to other descriptions from literature but to the memory of someone seen:

> We have seen her
> the world over,
>
> Our Lady of the Goldfinch,
> Our Lady of the Candelabra,
>
> Our Lady of the Pomegranate,
> Our Lady of the Chair;
>
> we have seen her, an empress,
> magnificent in pomp and grace, . . .
>
> the painters did very well by her;
> it is true, they missed never a line
>
> of the suave turn of the head
> or subtle shade of lowered eye-lid
>
> or eye-lids half-raised; you find
> her everywhere (or did find),
>
> in cathedral, museum, cloister,
> at the turn of the palace stair . . .
>
> But none of these, none of these
> suggest her as I saw her, . . .

For I can say truthfully,
her veils were *white as snow*,

*so as no fuller on earth
can white them*; I can say

she looked beautiful, she looked lovely,
she was *clothed with a garment*

down to the foot, but it was not
girt about with a golden girdle,

there was no gold, no colour,
there was no gleam in the stuff

nor shadow of hem or seam,
as it fell to the floor; she bore

none of her usual attributes;
the Child was not with her.
("Tribute to the Angels, *Selected Poems*, 89–93)

Purple, violets, amaranth, and similar references to
high spiritual content recur in H.D.'s work, as is true of
Sappho's fragments and, as I said, of Emily Dickinson's
poems. In one remarkable poem, "Amaranth," that seems
to be on the subject Lesbian love (but is probably about
her break-up with Richard Aldington), H.D. speaks in
Sappho's voice directly to Aphrodite:

Am I blind alas,
am I blind,
I too have followed her path.

I too have bent at her feet.
I too have wakened to pluck
amaranth in the straight shaft,
amaranth purple in the cup,
scorched at the edge to white . . .

Ah no—though I stumble toward
her altar-step,
though my flesh is scorched and rent,
shattered, cut apart,
and slashed open;
though my heels press my own wet life
black, dark to purple,
on the smooth rose-streaked
threshold of her pavement.[7]

She ends in tribute to Aphrodite:

Turn if you will from her path
for one moment seek
a lesser beauty
and a lesser grace,
but you will find
no peace in the end
save in her presence.

In her intense explorations on the nature of love, H.D.
made a remarkable discovery early on, in 1919, when she
described a different kind of intelligence than had been
previously defined: a "lovemind," she wrote in her jour-
nal, a "wombmind." This is from *Notes on Thought and*
Vision:

Vision is of two kinds—vision of the womb and vision of the brain.

In vision of the brain, the region of consciousness is above and about the head; when the center of consciousness shifts and the jelly-fish is in the body, (I visualize it in my case lying on the left side with the streamer or feelers floating up toward the brain) we have vision of the womb or love-vision.

The majority of dream and of ordinary vision is vision of the womb . . .

The brain and the womb are both centres of consciousness, equally important.[8]

"The brain and the womb are both centres of consciousness, equally important," what a marvelous idea! It is, in fact, a remarkably ancient idea, to say nothing of the tradition of the occult. Not until a well-developed "women's spirituality movement" emerged in the 1970s has there been much possibility of this idea taking root in contemporary society, or of H.D.'s work at last being understood by others than mystics and poets, her peers. She described the circumstances under which one could activate this "lovemind," saying that people without wombs could use the "love region" of their bodies in the absence of a womb.[9] (I prefer to call this "love region" the sex center.) H.D. said:

We must be "in love" before we can understand the mysteries of vision.

A lover must choose one of the same type of mind as himself, a musician, a musician, a scientist, a scientist, a general, a young man also interested in the theory and practice of arms and armies.

We begin with sympathy of thought.

The minds of the two lovers merge, interact in sympathy of thought.

The brain, inflamed and excited by this interchange of ideas, takes on its character of over-mind, becomes (as I have visualized in my own case) a jelly-fish, placed over and about the brain.

The love-region is excited by the appearance or beauty of the loved one, its energy not dissipated in physical relation, takes on its character of mind, becomes this womb-brain or love-brain that I have visualized as a jelly-fish in the body.

The love-brain and over-brain are both capable of thought.

This thought is vision.

All men[10] have possibilities of developing this vision. (*Notes on Thought and Vision*, 22)

She developed her visualization of the "jelly-fish" of consciousness of the brain and love-minds, she says, just prior to the birth of her child in March of 1919. She had undergone five years of stultifying unhappiness. Her first marriage, to Richard Aldington, was destroyed bitterly during the Great War that was one experience for men and another for women. Her body was torn by a miscarriage; during her second pregnancy, doctors predicted death for herself and her child. She sank into a pervasive depression that left her dulled and indifferent, apparently dying (though actually going through a transformation) in a dingy boardinghouse. There, the young, willful, loyal, completely-in-love Bryher found her and woke her to new feelings. The daughter of a shipping magnate, Bryher (Winifred Ellerman) had the personal capacity to inherit and run the company. Instead, as the daughter, she turned her willfulness toward her writing and toward supporting innovative writers around her: James Joyce, for example, and especially H.D. (though H.D. actually had plenty of money of her own). Bryher, whose father H.D. described as Jewish, spent her money on liberal causes. She was evidently scorned—probably jealously—by male admirers of H.D.'s extraordinary beauty. Bryher's later photographs show a butchy woman with extremely short hair wearing man-type suits. H.D. described her small, strange companion as a little gray gull, an elf.

That's life,
but I had grown accustomed
to disappointment,
insecurity, gloom;

I begged for a place in their room
I, a shadow, sought a place
where disgrace attended . . .

O what, what, what

sent you, all grey, unnoticeable
and small
to shatter my peace,
unconscionable little gull?
("Halcyon," *Notes on Thought and Vision*, 271–72)

Bryher took her to the Scilly Islands off Cornwall and in July, just weeks after their relationship began, H.D.

wrote her remarkable descriptions of the "love-mind." The new understanding of vision happened to her, she said, just prior to the birth of her child; that is, just as Bryher entered her life. It is a special mind, a mind of vision that could best be entered, she said, by like-minded people. Her examples imply love between homosexual men, for what other relationship during that time would involve a general and a soldier? She does not explicitly name a Lesbian pair bond, yet as "writer with writer" describes herself and Bryher, and it was certainly during the first excitement of their love-bond that her insights about the "love-brain" came to her—perhaps in some such circumstances as is described in this poem from her series on Bryher, "Halcyon":

You say, "lie still";
your hand is chill,
cold, unimpassioned,
inviolable;

you say, "lie back,
you won't faint";
what makes you think that?
what makes you think

I won't drift out,
get quite away?

(276)

Quarreling was a great part of the feelings let loose by the emotionally awakened H.D., and she ends "Halcyon" with this:

190

we quarrel again—
don't talk—dismiss happiness,
unhappiness, pain, bliss,
even thought—

what's left?
imcomparable beyond belief,
white stones
immaculate sand,

the slow move-forward of the tide
on a shallow reef,
salt and dried weed,
the wind's low hiss;

it's here in my skull
(leave your hand there)
for you—for ever—
mysterious little gull

(277)

It's clear from her poetry that what H.D. sought and got from Bryher was a steadfast foundation in reality. From this island she reached into the deepest levels of the "real dream," finding there an old goddess of love, beauty, intelligence, and vision.

God As What We Do

Even as she defined the goddess who appeared to her in vision and dream, and the one who hid in Egypt rather than participating in the war at Troy, H.D. also stayed alert to the tribulations of the world. "Like Bryher, who helped more than 100—mostly Jewish—refugees escape Nazi Germany between 1933 and 1939, H.D. was deeply anti-Fascist, finally cutting off all ties" with poet friend Ezra Pound "because of his pro-Fascist stance" ("H.D. 1886–1991," Poetry Foundation).

The two women acted in an antiracist 1930 film: "Testifying to the influence of the Harlem Renaissance on H.D., *Borderline* is a full-length feature film about interracial sex and violence, starring Paul and Essie Robeson, along with H.D. and Bryher. The essay entitled *Borderline* that H.D. published about the film demonstrates how important issues of racial discrimination and African-American culture were to the formation of her postwar modernist vision" ("H.D. 1886–1961," Poetry Foundation).

All the contemporary Lesbian poets were antiracist and antiwar, though not anti-self-defense; poets attended demonstrations against the Vietnam War, supported the activism of the Black Panthers, and participated in or led all manner of feminist activist projects. Like Pat Parker, we walked our talk. But political activism and engagement with people's struggles in the crises of their lives are completely central to the works of Pat Parker. What much of Parker's work demands is that we pay attention to injustice, and as such she embodies the ethical and compassionate principles without which spirituality alone is hollow.

"Don't let the fascists speak," Pat concluded her poem "I am a child of America" about a controversy over free speech and a Nazi speaker: "it is illegal / to scream fire / in a crowded theater . . . / causes people to panic / to run to hurt each other" (*Collected Works*, 71). Of the many bitter ironies of racial segregation, she was especially offended by a flooded Southern town whose people could not bury their dead because no one could tell the difference between Black and white bodies, and the two cemeteries were strictly separated ("Sunday," 64). About contemporary oppression, Pat described new chains, "chains lying strange / chains lying lightweight . . . lying no jobs . . . chains lying ignorance . . . lying fear . . . how do I break these chains" (88).

Her background included two sets of African American grandparents who had been enslaved, and on her mother's side, a great-grandmother who was Caddo Indian, a community that had long lived in what would become Texas. From growing up in segregated Houston, Pat fled to California, married and divorced two men by age twenty-four, and came out as a Lesbian, probably in 1969. She realized herself as a Lesbian in a Gay bar on a visit to Houston, and therefore, she said, as a joke on herself, that she thought cowboy clothes were "Gay clothes," so at first she wore boots, vest, cowboy shirt, and hat. "All black of course," she told me with a big grin. I got it: cowboys come in "good or bad," depending on whether the hat is white or black, so Pat was challenging the (white supremacist) notion of "good" by wearing black cowboy clothes.

Like the rest of us poets, Pat was in hot demand for readings that helped bring her multiple communities together, with words that focused people's attention on issues just as her words also mirrored them to themselves. Though she herself did not say this to me, I believe that Pat's major work and unrelenting focus on justice were fed not only by her own often horrific experiences, but also by three murders of people close to her. Pat's poem "my brother" is dedicated to her Gay friend Black-berri Singer, who would occasionally visit, eat, stay over-night. They wouldn't talk much, but his silence "alerts me / tells me this time / is hard time / the pain has risen / to the water line." To know what her friend faced she only needed to recall her teenage friend Claude, their family's paperboy, who always showed up no matter how muddy their neighborhood with its absence of sidewalks; he was such a good person her stern father allowed her to go to the junior prom with him. But Claude was always called anti-Gay names, and one day neighborhood boys robbed him, beat him, and threw him in front of a car to his death (195).

A second murder, the femicide of Pat's older sister Shirley after separating from her husband, occurred in 1970 and led Pat to write in response her powerful long poem *Womanslaughter*. The killer, "a quiet man," wounded Shirley's best friend as well, yet was given a light sentence, a year of working during the day, sleeping in the jail at night. His white boss had testified, "He works well for me." Pat detailed the response of the family, how glad she was that their father wasn't alive to witness the traves-ty of justice: "He would surely kill the quiet man." How helpless Shirley's surviving sisters felt in the face of the judge's betrayal, his calling this a crime of passion: "Men don't kill their wives," the poem rages, "They *passion* them to death." She ends *Womanslaughter*, as I said ear-lier, with a vow to defend endangered women by gathering all her feminist sisters to protect the vulnerable: "I will come strong" (*Collected Works*, 149). Powerful words, and courts did hand out more appropriate sentences after much protesting. But femicide remains a national—and worldwide—atrocity.

The third murder happened early in her life. Pat told me how as a child she learned from her mother that Pat's uncle Dave's "suicide" while in jail was no suicide: this was murder, that is to say, a form of lynching by police. The violent seventies in the US saw a great many targeted attacks against the Black Panthers and other activists, infiltration and undermining of feminist institutions, and the assassination of the first openly Gay elected official, Harvey Milk in SF. But nothing could approach the horror of the mass murders in November of 1978 of over 900 mostly Black people, at the hands of a power- and drug-crazed white authoritarian, Jim Jones.

Meticulously, Parker crafted in her poem "Jonestown" an analysis of the steps to a false hope and then helplessness that led people to stay in an increasingly abusive cult, staking everything on a dangerous utopian ideal that ended in unbelievable mass death by cyanide. The long poem chronicles society's abuses and neglect that can lead vulnerable people to become trapped in such an imprisoned environment. The poem's chorus pounds its message: "Black folks do not / Black folks do not / Black folks do not commit suicide" (Collected Works, 227). I think Pat's early understanding of her uncle's death as murder gave her the focused motivation to write such a powerful poem about the massacre.

Pat never wavered in her support for her communities, serving ten years as Executive Director of the Oakland Feminist Women's Health Center. She tirelessly pushed women's issues forward and wrote "Movement in Black" as a paeon of praise for Black women, ordinary as "I'm the teacher . . . I'm the social worker . . . I'm the car hop . . . I'm the matron at a county jail," renowned as "Phyllis

Wheatley, Sojourner Truth, Harriet Tubman," and more contemporarily, "Angela Davis . . . Zora Neale Hurston . . . Nikki Giovanni." She punctuated the performance poem with a pulsing chorus:

> movement in Black
> movement in Black
> can't keep 'em back
> movement in Black
>
> (98)

In contrast to the other poets I am discussing, she did not describe or name goddesses, spiritual visions, or even make many references to nature. However, her poem "For Willyce," besides being outrageously funny, is also quite on point:

> when I make love to you
>   I try
>   with each stroke of my tongue
>   to say   I love you
>   to tease   I love you
>   to hammer   I love you
>   to melt   I love you
>
>   & your sounds drift down
>   oh god!
>   oh Jesus!
>   and I think—
> here it is, some dude's
> getting credit for what
>   a woman

has done,
     again

(110)

In one of the most beautiful of love poems, Pat expressed the feminist ideal; "Right Relationship" is certainly a major teaching of spirituality, and Pat wrote about equality in human partnership directly:

Let me come to you naked
come without my masks
come dark
        and lay beside you

Let me come to you old
come as a dying snail
come weak
        and lay beside you

Let me come to you angry
come shaking with hate
come callused
        and lay beside you

even more

Let me come to you strong
come sure and free
 come powerful

and lay with you.

(126)

For the lover to arrive without masks and to lay beside and then *with* the beloved rather than on top of or underneath hearkens to Lillith's rebellion against the "missionary position" required by Adam. The poem also describes what Gay cultural leader Harry Hay called subject-subject relationships. Carried into society at large, this is a liberatory approach. Not for nothing was Pat's nickname in her broad Lesbian community, if not also beyond, "The Preacher."

Paula Gunn Allen used a cosmology drawn from American Indian and modern "Sethian" understanding of the physical world as not only alive, but malleable, responding to our expressed desires. Our gods can be seen, she says, by looking at how we order our world, at *what we do*. In a poem, "Taku skan-skan," she has put this idea to words:

> that history is an event
> that life is
> that I am event
> ually to go do something
> the metaphor for god.
> eventuality.
> activity.

> what happens   to *be*
> what happens   to *me*
> god. history. action.
> the Lakota word for it is:
> *what movesmoves.*
> they don't call god "what moves something."
> not "prime mover,"

"first mover," "who moves everything or nothing,"
"action," "lights," or "movement."
not "where" or "what" or 'how," but
event. GOD
is what happens, is:
movesmoves.

riding a mare.
eventuality.
out of the corral into morning
taking her saddled and bridled
air thick with breath movesmoves
horsebreath, mybreath, earthbreath,
skybreathing air. ing.
breathesbreathes   movesmoves
in the cold. winterspringfall.
corral.   ing.   horse and breath.
air. through the gate moveswe.
lift we the wooden crossbar *niya*
movesmoves unlocks movesbreathes
lifebreath of winter soul
swings wide sweet corral gate
happens to be frozenstiff in place
happens to be cold. so I and mare
wear clothes that move in event
of frozen. shaggy hair dressers for the air
breathes breathe we: flows: movesmoves:
god its cold
no other place but movesmoves
horse me gate hinge air bright frost lungs
swing gate out far morning winter rides
movesmovingmoves Lakota words: god.
what we do.[11]

Gods from Non-Western Worlds

As early as 1970, Audre Lorde began pulling godstuff from the African and Afro-American traditions into her work. In "The Winds of Orisha," she begins, "This land will not always be foreign."[12] The poem speaks of Tiresias, the Greek figure who "took 100 years to grow into a woman / so do not despair of your sons." It then continues with descriptions of the major Macumba gods, who are called the "Orisha": Yemanja, Oshun, Oya, Shango, and Eshu. This pantheon was retained in North and South America by enslaved Africans who mixed the religion with some American Indian gods and customs, then, in Brazil especially, coated it all with a thin Catholic veneer for camouflage:

> Mother Yemanja raises her breasts to begin my labor
> near water
> the beautiful Oshun and I lie down together
> in the heat of her body truth my voice comes stronger
> Shango will be my brother roaring out of the sea
> earth shakes our darkness swelling into each other
> warming winds will announce us living
> as Oya, Oya my sister my daughter
> destroys the crust of the tidy beaches
> and Eshu's black laughter turns up the neat sleeping sand.
> (48–49)

Eshu is the eternal trickster of the crossroads, highly phallic and somewhat resembling American Indian Coyote and ancient tribal god Hermes in his raucous and chaotic functions of disrupting the fixed order of belief.

Yemanja is the Great Mother of the Sea; Oshun is Beauty, the Evening Star, and inland waters, the lake. Oya, to whom Lorde devoted another full poem on the subject of anger, and who she calls "my sister my daughter," is the storm goddess, a warrior supreme, unafraid of the spirits of the dead. Her brother is Shango, who received his tools—his battle ax—from her.

I believe it was following a trip Lorde made throughout west Africa in the early or mid-seventies that she added to these Yoruba gods from a second African-based pantheon, the Vodu from Dahomey, or Dan, as the ancient, powerful culture center was called formerly.

Gods of both regions constitute the group she prays to and through in *The Black Unicorn*. In these poems she successfully transfers them to New York streets and sees them in the persons of modern urban Americans in a manner similar to that used by Sappho when she describes the qualities of love and beauty in the persons of women she loves. Similarly, the Native American poet Joy Harjo acknowledges the deity of the Moon by calling her "last one out of a bar in Albuquerque";[13] and in *The Queen of Wands*, I locate Helen in a factory and as a factory. The point is that deity does not live in the remote heavens, nor stay hidden and exclusive in cloisters and grottoes, no matter how appealing. The godpower must come out and be present with us where we are, where we live and act and feel, here in concrete and plastic, in airplanes and freeways and tenements and brutality and cancer and chemical addictions and need and threat of nuclear war. Here is where we shall find, locate, and establish the gods that might help us on this continent of mixtures and dishevelment, to make them feel at home.

Audre Lorde addresses her gods forcefully and naturally, as in "125th Street and Abomey" (Abomey is the capital of Dahomey):

Head bent, walking through snow
I see you Seboulisa
printed inside the back of my head . . .
Seboulisa mother goddess with one breast
eaten away by worms of sorrow and loss
see me now
your severed daughter
laughing our name into echo
all the world shall remember.[14]

Like Paula Gunn Allen with her Indian traditions, Lorde is able to translate the details of her life into mythic terms. For instance, in "From the House of Yemanja":

My mother had two faces and a frying pot
where she cooked up her daughters
into girls
before she fixed our dinner.
My mother had two faces
and a broken pot
where she hid out a perfect daughter
who was not me

(6)

Of particular importance to the work of understanding and developing new Lesbian archetypes is Lorde's surfacing with the Black woman warrior, of whom she names several. The storm god Oya we have met, with her thunders and her winds and rain. Afrikete is most well-developed in Lorde's biomythography, *Zami*; Afrikete is a trickster, a changer, a mysterious and lavish lover, a singer, and a poet. Colossa is a dancer, appearing in the poem "Scar" as a "big black woman with jewels in her eyes . . . her head in a golden helmet/arrogant/plumed . . . / her thighs are like stanchions," and at the shiny edge of her metal tunic, "an astonishment of black curly hair" (48–50).

And finally, "The Women of Dan Dance with Swords in Their Hands to Mark the Time When They Were Warriors" is both the name of a poem and a description of the line of African Amazons who served the Panther Kings of Dahomey. In her American context and in Lorde's hands, the African Amazon is a unification of anger and love, resolution, and affirmation, transformed purposefully out of the era of enslavement:

> I do not come like a secret warrior
> with an unsheathed sword in my mouth
> hidden behind my tongue
> slicing my throat to ribbons
> of service with a smile
> while the blood runs down and out
> through holes in the two sacred mounds
> on my chest.
>
> I come like a woman
> who I am
> spreading out through nights
> laughter and promise
>
> (14–15)

By connecting her life, and by extension all of our lives, to the ancient and still underlying tribal life, to the communitas of rite and of gods, Lorde is helping us to gain meaning on a plane far greater than the everyday drudge of physical activity. Dickinson called this entering the "Drama, and Drama never dies." Sappho called it being connected to the House of the Muses, and that those who failed to do so would be forgotten, even among the dead. H.D. called it the "real dream." Lorde calls it "Our name," and "memory," messages brought to us through the magic office and voice of a special contemporary unicorn, the Black unicorn.

Having a mythic history with genuine godforces operating on daily level is completely necessary to the Lesbian poetic search for what Mary Carruthers calls a new Lesbian *civitas*, a paradigm, a model of a new community, a new relationship of women to the world.

Sappho had an integrated religious ceremonial/mythological matrix to draw from, one shared by all her audience, not only a "common language" with common dreams, but also with common gods. Our tradition is fragmented, actually fractured, and each of the Lesbian poets of our era is drawing from a completely different tradition for her naming and defining of her gods. Even Olga Broumas, a native Greek, who naturally draws from the Greek mythology of her land of origin, alters the stories so drastically as to render them unrecognizable to Sappho's ancient world.

But Broumas's act is necessary for the restructuring, for the old tales have been dissembled to the disadvantage of women. Broumas is in the tradition of Sappho, therefore, when she re-feminizes and revitalizes the old names, as in "Twelve Aspects of God" wherein all twelve are female—Circe, Demeter, Artemis, Calypso. Here is the second part of "Amazon Twins":

In the gazebo-like cafe, you gave
me food from your plate, alert
to my blood-sweet hungers
double edged
in the glare of the sun's
and our own
twin heat. Yes, there
we were, breasts on each side, Amazons
adolescent at twentynine
privileged
to keep the bulbs and to feel the blade
swell, breath-sharp
on either side. In that public place

in that public place.[15]

Caritas and Beginning with O define a Lesbian sexuality that is sacred, aware, has a mythic history and is totally present. As critic Mary Carruthers puts it:

Innocence, play, sentience, and familiarity are the marks of Broumas' erotic language. Her love poetry desires not *raptus*, the loss of self, but depicts union through recognition, through images of choir, dance, laughter, touch, of diverse yet familiar voices making sweet harmony. The tongue, organ of speech and consciousness, which in romantic tradition is opposite and inadequate to the desired unconscious *raptus* of sexual union, is in this new context an instrument both of sex and consciousness. In that fortunate Lesbian correspondence, Broumas lays the foundation of her myth[16]

And in her myth god is female, is varied, is familiar, and is sapphically erotic, as in "Innocence," where the poet finds,

with the glide of a tongue, a hand
precise as an eyelid, a hand with a sense
of smell, a hand that will dance
to its liquid moan.
God's hand
(*Beginning with O*, 45–47)

In a later book, *Pastoral Jazz*, a book that never fails to give me some happiness, Broumas has gone into a subterranean level, a starting over that repeats the sensation of something beautiful, sad, and fierce that is busy being born of a shallow green sea with lavender shadows. "The child goes underground, whirling and fainting," she says in "Sea Change."[17]

Broumas in *Pastoral Jazz* is no longer naming, she is unnaming. Naming and re-naming are only two of our chores. Another is unnaming, as is found in Gertrude Stein, Paula Gunn Allen, and in my own "She Who" poems and novel *Mundane's World*. *Pastoral Jazz* leaves both name and story behind to enter language, still erotic, as everything Broumas's pen touches is infused with Lesbian sexuality and a women's aesthetic that is holy, and wholly physical.

Delta and Delta to the touch
Nile streaming *open open*
Open of opens
which sun sings? which sea
stiff nippled curly measures?

(45)

In poetry of language and the body, what is imparted
is impression and essential rhythm, as when birds talk.
What is imparted is no longer rigid, defined, structured,
superimposed, or mandatory. It is *calling* rather than
naming; and the emotions can include delight, humor,
and the sublimely ludicrous as well as the seriously beau-
tiful, the sexual, and the sacred.

In this scheme, small things are what matters:

No choice but a gradual ascent, the silkworm's
passage to Byzantium from China, deliberate loss of all
heroism, even in pleasure. Hammock cords
shake in the light. You sit down
to a common meal, raw carrots,
lettuce, radishes, olives and other things, a place
both empty and set.

(25)

And in this scheme, Venus is always being re-born from
the sea, everything is beginning, and the apple is found to
have seeds:

If I think along
the stations of the day
how observe them?

Sweet apples
Mild chill of fall
harvested and resown seeds
Always to be beginning!
(56)

Godmind, Godforce, Godlove

None of the Lesbian poets under discussion concentrate on one female divinity, as in the sense of "The Goddess," or even, "The Mother," and write to her; all of us are pantheistic.

Yet even calling Adrienne Rich "pantheistic" may seem absurd given that she has never, to my knowledge, named in the magic of her poetry a goddess, or addressed her, or even mentioned her in passing. And yet she names the forces, the female godforces, and takes as her major subjects love and beauty, intelligence and memory—surely Aphrodite or perhaps the Hebrew Asherah—in another form. Moreover, Rich writes, like the rest of us, in a metaphysical time frame, sure sign of a seer connected to what occultists and spiritualists call "the higher mind," the one that is eons old, the one with the long and sacred memory.

Speaking out of the mouth of the brilliant painter Paula Becker, who died in childbirth in 1907, Rich says:

I have the feeling I'm
moving somewhere, patiently, impatiently,
in my loneliness. I'm looking everywhere in nature
for new forms, old forms in new places,
the planes of an antique mouth, let's say, among the leaves.
I know and do not know

what I am searching for.[18]

And in "Nights and Days" she has her eye on a certain flower, a hyacinth (was it the one Sappho said the shepherds trampled in the mountains, twenty-five hundred years ago?). "The stars will come out over and over / the hyacinths rise like flames / from the windswept turf down the middle of upper Broadway"—this hyacinth is located in the center of the city; she continues,

We are holding hands so I can see
everything as you see it
I follow you into your dreams
your past, the places
none of us can explain to anyone.
(45)

And then she describes the lover's sleep as "sacred." The sun is female, the city is "wrapped in her indestructible light." The poem "Sibling Mysteries" is a chronicle of the recognition of two sisters recalling the long history of women as the daughters of the mother: "piecing our lore in quilted galaxies" (49). And, so beautifully in "Twenty-One Love Poems," she describes the godspirit as "nameless till we rename her":

XI

Every peak is a crater. This is the law of volcanoes,
making them eternally and visibly female.
No height without depth, without a burning core,
though our straw soles shred on the hardened lava.
I want to travel with you to every sacred mountain

smoking within like the sibyl stooped over her tripod,
I want to reach for your hand as we scale the path,
to feel your arteries glowing in my clasp,
never failing to note the small, jewel-like flower
unfamiliar to us, nameless till we rename her,
that clings to the slowly altering rock—
that detail outside ourselves that brings us to ourselves,
was here before us, knew we would come, and sees beyond us
(30)

Each of the contemporary Lesbian poets has drawn from the myth of an "ideal place," a new island from which to center a civilized, graceful, loving culture that has passion and physical substance as well as metaphysical and psychic substance. In Lorde's work, this ideal place is sometimes "Dahomey," or even more anciently, "Dan." In Broumas, it is the sea, as well as the lovers' arms, a place of continual rebirth. Sappho used Lesbos as an ideal place, speaking of the poets of Lesbos as the best and herself as best of the best.

In her poem "Sources," Adrienne Rich locates an ideal place from a Jewish context:

XXI

YERUSHALAYIM: a vault of golden heat
hard-pulsing from bare stones

the desert's hard-won, delicate green
the diaspora of the stars

thrilling like thousand-year-old locusts
audible yet unheard

a city on a hill
waking with first light to voices

piercing, original, intimate
as if my dreams mixed with the cries

of the oldest, earliest birds
and of all whose wrongs and rights

cry out for explication
as the night pales and one more day

breaks on this *Zion* of hope and fear
and broken promises
this promised land[19]

Each poet has located the place of wholeness and the
method of approaching it—each location is specific to
the background, ethnicity, and experience of the poet,
yet each place applies as well to all people. Yerushalayim
is Rich's Jewish/American metaphor for "the city on the
hill," the ideal civilization. And the "diaspora of the stars"
is not only a reference to the Jewish diaspora, but also
the scattering of our various ancestral origins, of dreams
that have become—not ashes—but stars. Stars. Hopes.
Worlds. Renewals.

As for the godstuff in my own work, the "She Who"
poems were the first of my poems that I thought of as
conjure poems. I think of them as that because not only
are they using strongly physical imagery, but they are
also using strong rhythms that call the thing to itself with
images and sounds. They were deliberately aimed at a

physical part of the body, to trigger a particular response in the human body. I knew I was getting the words close to the feeling/state I wanted to conjure for each poem if a little gland in my throat went off when I read the poem to myself—a little spit gland, probably, with a sharp pang attached to it. If this gland went off, I knew the poem was a finished "She Who" poem and I added it to the stack, which begins with lines like: "who who SHE, she-who, she WHO-WHO?" (Work of a Common Woman, 77).

I did not know about chakras at that time, the little energy wheels whirling at certain parts of our bodies—the tailbone area, sexual area, solar plexus, heart, throat, third eye, and top of the head. Probably the little throat gland that I aimed the "She Who" poems at is the physical correlative of the throat chakra. Like Gertrude Stein, I was attempting to surround the subject of female godforce without naming it. In 1972 when the series was written, the Lesbian feminist movement around me was still nearly completely materialist in its orientation, suspicious of all things religious. Besides, hadn't I also spent years scorning spirituality?

Additionally, I would not have known what name to use; I have never liked the word goddess because it seems to be a diminutive of the word "god" and not an active principle on its own account. I recognize hundreds of forces, spirits, shadows, gods, goblins, and fairies, as well as major female and male gods who, in my life, have taken a variety of forms. I cannot imagine consolidating all that variety of form and pulse into monotheism.

But in "Confrontations with the Devil in the Form of Love," Love is personified in a direct manner, and "the

Devil" is a form of Sappho, of women's fractured sexual being, and by extension the whole sunken antique world that underlies our Western history, that has been burnt and misshapen.

> My name is Judith, meaning
> She Who Is Praised
> I do not want to be called praised
> I want to be called The Power of Love.
>
> if Love means protect then whenever I do not
> defend you
> I cannot call my name Love.
> if Love means rebirth then when I see us
> dead on our feet
> I cannot call my name Love
> if Love means provide & I cannot
> provide for you
> why would you call my name Love?[20]

The re-naming of Love is brought forward most strongly in "A Woman Is Talking to Death." There, the "death-myth" of the old patriarchal system is juxtaposed to the ability of any kinds of "lovers" to defend each other against it, and to band together in another place:

> we are the fat of the land, and
> we all have our list of casualties
>
> to my lovers I bequeath
> the rest of my life.
> (130)

In the "Confrontations" poem, "My name is Judith," the re-naming of Love involves calling for its power out in the world, a power not yet realized ("do not mistake my breasts for mounds of potatoes . . . nor take my feet to be acres of solid brown earth" [157]). Most importantly, don't mistake for "romance" the Love the poet is asking us all to seek. Don't mistake Love for escape, for the security of the couple bond that compensates for all we do not have of love and autonomy, of choice and definition, of power and the sacredness of our beings, in the world at large. Let us take on the world at large and recreate these things within it. Love is being named now, in poems, poems that mock Love's fall from power as merely Venus, the head-less body of a statue:

Venus dear, where are your arms?
if only you were a tree.
they have so many
& no one thinks less of them for it.
(146)

Love is being named, personified, and confronted with the limitations that have been placed on her, is being asked to become more, much, much more. She is being openly addressed, as Aphrodite was openly addressed by Sappho, but here she has an American name, an Anglo-Saxon name, Love. Her powers are her "apples." She has a different history, has been a "devil," has been a sex-toy, a Venus, has been "simply romance" (135–58). As this "Devil," which is less-than-herself, she is being confronted in the poems. She is being asked to transform her functions now, to include protection, provision, and power, and to be out in the world with us, as our partner.

Love, combined with intelligence and beauty, at last joined together in my poetry and in my understanding in *The Queen of Wands*. Adrienne Rich in her introduction to my first collection of poetry had gotten me interested in a poet I had previously considered too classical for me to understand: H.D. Between *Helen in Egypt* and a line of Rich's about "loving with all my intelligence," I came to some stories of Helen as a stolen god, a god of creativity and of the old weaving powers. These women's weaving powers have been deified on this continent as well, for instance in the person of the Pueblo Indian creatrix, Spider Grandmother. Helen, as the goddess of love, creation, weaving, fire, and beauty, is a form of Aphrodite: beauty as intelligent creativity, love as a form of envisioning, envisioning with a psychic/sexual mind. The Helen poems in *The Queen of Wands* place her majesty squarely in the world, the everyday American workaday world, as the "egg of being," the dream of America itself, and the voice describing her as such is an ancient one, the deep one underneath in the purple shadows, Spider Webster.

Helen
you always were
the egg laid
by the golden goose,
the full pot, the fat purse,
the best bet, the sure horse
the Christmas rush
the bundle he's about to make;
the gold mine, a house of our own
the ship come in, the next stake,
the nest egg, the big deal, the steal—

215

the land of opportunity
the lovely lady being
luck and love and lust
and the last chance
for any of us,
the reason that he's living
for, Helen you're always
high card, ace in the hole and
more, the most, the first and best,
the sun
burst
goodness   quenching every thirst
the girl of the golden golden golden
West,
desire that beats
in every chest

heart of the sky

and some bizarre
dream substance
we pave streets with
here in America[21]

And in that book of poems (which is the first of four
books chronicling queens from the Tarot and other
sources), Love/Beauty/Mind in the form of the stolen Helen
promises to return in her rightful position as Mother of
the People. The second book, *The Queen of Swords*, will
undertake definition and re-cognition of the warrior, the
quintessential Dyke. From the research I have done, and
from knowing the habits of Lesbians, and from under-

standing that the warrior she-god of ancient and tribal times has been a wielder of storms, and a lover of her powers, I have written the following poem or verse of a poem:

Lesbians love to dance / inside the thunder

Lesbians love to dance
outside in the rain
with lightning darting
all around them. Lesbians
love to dance together
in the pouring rain, in
summer.
Lesbians love to dance
inside the thunder,
sheets of water
washing over their whole bodies
and the dark clouds
boiling and roiling like a
giant voice calling.
Lesbians love to answer
voices calling like that.
Lesbians love to
dance without their clothing
in thunderstorms with
lightning as their partner.
Screaming, holding hands
and turning soaking faces
skyward in tumultuous
noise and yearning. Lesbians
love to see each other

learning to completely
rejoice. Lesbians love
to feel the power
and the glory they can dance
inside of, in a storm
of their communal choice.[22]

The pantheon of Paula Gunn Allen, as it has developed in her work, includes the Laguna Pueblo female creator gods, especially Grandmother Spider, who is also called Thought Woman, and her sister, the Mother of the People, Corn Woman, or Iyatiku. Allen's "biomythography," to use Audre Lorde's apt word, is *The Woman Who Owned the Shadows*. Stories of the Indigenous gods, especially female gods, figure prominently, giving the protagonist ways to make a meaning of her life in our fractured modern American society.

Although weaving, especially weaving the universe from her own substance, is a primary quality of Allen's creatrix, water is Allen's major image of grace. Sappho, too, used liquid imagery most often to describe her gods' behaviors. They pour golden nectars and wines, fill cups and jugs, while cold water babbles through apple-branches in the sacred groves. She speaks of dewy banks, of dews shed in beauty, of ambrosia in bowls, and intriguingly, of a dripping wet napkin.

Perhaps it is only natural from a native of the great desert of the Southwest, as Allen is, and a registered member of a community calling itself Laguna, "Lake," that she would say of rain, "So when it rains everyone is whole, you know that god loves you."[23]

Allen uses water in describing her coming out into the world of Lesbianism as it has manifested itself in America for the last decade, and of coming out into a con-sciousness of the possible bonds and beauty, the possible love and wisdom, of all women. The following lines are from a poem called "He Na Tye Woman" (Female Rain Woman):

> Water (woman) that is the essense of you
> He na tye (woman) that is recognition
> > and remembering.
> Gentle. Soft. Sure.
> Water (woman) that is the essense of you
> He na tye (woman) that is recognition
> > and remembering.
> Gentle. Soft. Sure.
> Long shadows of afternoon, growing
> > as the light turns
> west toward sleep. Turning with the sun.
> (The rest of it is continents and millennia.
> (How could I have waited so long for completion?)
>
> The water rises around us like the goddess
> > coming home.
> (Arisen.) Some trip, all things considered,
> > all times
> and visions, all places and spaces taken
> > into account
> on that ancient journey, finally returned.
> > The maps, the plans,
> the timetables: the carefully guided tours
> > into all manner
> of futilities. Manners the last turn in the road:
> > arid irony.

(Lady, why does your love so touch me?)
(Lady, why do my hands have strength for you?)
(Lady, how could I wander so long without you?)

Water in Falls, misting and booming on the
                              rocks below.
Tall pines in the mist, the deep carved caves.
Water in rivulets. Gathering speed, drops joining
                              in headlong
flight.
Unnamed rivers, flowing eternally underground,
                              unchanging, unchanged.
Water thundering down long dry arroyos,
                         the ancient causeways
of our faith. Drought over, at last. Carrying silt,
bits of broken glass, branches, pebbles, pieces of
                              abandoned cars,
parts of lost houses and discarded dreams.
                         Downstream.
Storms of water, and we
deluged
singing
hair plastered to our ecstatic skulls,
waving wild fists at the bolts hurled at us
                         from above
teeth shimmering in the sheets of rain
                    (the sheen)
eyes blinded with the torrents that
                    fall fromthroughover
                    them:

Rain. The Rain that makes us new.

That rain is you.
How did I wait so long to drink.[24]

God, at Laguna, is female, is Spider Grandmother, Thought Woman. The legend says that she went away after the people stopped following her rituals. In Allen's work she is called forth again, in a more modern and out-in-the-world form—and through the bonding of women together. "Recognition and remembering" are the qualities the "grandlady" god has in He Na Tye Woman. In "Transitions," the poet makes even more explicit her return and the place of Lesbian love in her re-calling:

how you loved me. made love to me.
what i saw there when i was held.
in the wild tangle of our tongues' necessity,
rooting in softleafed places,
melting and pouring like the hills today,
ground gone to water, running toward the sea,
heat rising but not in rage.
in love.
just the seagray of your gaze,
your longing, arms raised to clasp
me,
  in sight
    of the Woman
  she
    lying in a pond
      in the woods
    in the pond of her self,
        her dreams.
  lying breathless, she

taken with a dream
a sighting of her
lovely lover
        who is coming down,
                        running down
to meet her where she's waiting
in her pond, in her lake, in her sea.
we could see her waiting
        for the time to be
                her time.
    her arms ready to rise
    her knees beginning to open, to lift,
we said: she's waking to love.

the woman whose waking means
wonder.
water.
want and need.
and her awakening is not death or war, not rage.
she's in love, that woman the world. she's in love.[25]

It is striking to me to realize that none of the gods described, named, addressed in our poetry is omnipotent. Audre Lorde specifies in the notes in *The Black Unicorn* that the Orisha are not omnipotent, are not even always just. Similarly, the gods of Paula Gunn Allen's world always need the participation of the human beings to complete their activity. As Rich says in her description of the flower who is a small detail outside ourselves and has, somehow, always known where we are going—the godstuff, the godhead and the godfoot and the godmind and the godsex and the godlove are within us as well as without us. We are an active, intelligent *part* of what is sacred, even a necessary part, as is everything else.

The feminist spiritual writer Starhawk speaks of this definition of deity in her article "Consciousness, Politics, and Magic," in *The Politics of Women's Spirituality*:

> Estrangement permeates our society so thoroughly that to us it seems to *be* consciousness itself; even the language for other possibilities has disappeared or been deliberately twisted. Yet, another form of consciousness is possible, indeed, has existed from earliest times. It underlies other cultures and has survived even in the West in hidden streams. This is the consciousness called *immanence*—the awareness of the world and everything in it as alive, dynamic, interdependent, and interacting, infused with moving energies: a living being, a weaving dance.[26]

In reclaiming and renaming the "confiscated gods," as Dickinson called them, we are also involving the reclamation of the "city," civitas, civilization with "caritas," as Broumas calls love. The place, the placenta, the connection to the Mother of Everything, as it is called by all of us; the unique and very female "heaven" of Dickinson; the white island of H.D.'s mind that is not Lesbianism but is a place of the power of women;[27] Laguna, the lake of healing waters of Allen; Dahomey, the ancient center of Dan of Lorde; Yerushalayim, land of promises and broken promises of Adrienne Rich; "the egg of being," the golden dream of America for me—where the egg is the dream immanent and the tree, the weaving tree, is the dream manifested. The place where we can be decent to each other, in commonality. Where the culture trance of oppositions is broken. Where there is some measure of safety, though as Rich says, "not anesthesia," not an "insured, guaranteed life." A place where the usual strident, linear oppositions no longer prevail because we shall have made a larger metaphor that incorporates the oppositional one within it. We shall have made a womb, or heart-shaped metaphor.

Describing the New Center

Defining and describing and uncovering a new or restored creation myth is in large measure what we are doing. In her article describing Lesbian poetry, Mary Carruthers says we have moved beyond revolution, into a longer arena, "eschatology," the final end of things—transformation of all things by transforming the words for them. She says,

> Eschatology, however, requires utter change, the end of all things as we know them, a new heaven and a new earth. It is a natural historical perspective for mystics and seers, for all those who by inclination and necessity do not vest their interest wholly in society but remain always in some way apart. The fact of her permanent estrangement is an essential ingredient of the Lesbian myth in its relationship to tradition, history and the poetic process.[28]

What we are doing, she says, is re-mythologizing our society, establishing a new *civitas*, a Lesbian civility, using the image, the metaethic of integrity, wholeness. *Civitas* originally meant the body of the citizens, the community. Only later did it come to mean the physical place, the city, the buildings and the streets. In medieval times, it was the community of believers on earth, with the City of God located in another place, away, in heaven.

The Lesbian *civitas*, community, is located here in the world of cold and hot factuality, here in a place that is the fragrant and stinking mother-place; that is, it is here with everything that it is. And it is here in the middle of the current fragmented, alienated patriarchal world. But the new *civitas* is here with its spiritual connections intact, here with its mysticism and its forces intact. It is here in bondings with familiars and an overlapping of commonality even in differences; here in a bond of community whose definitions can be indefinitely expanded as long as the principles of central integration, of factuality rather than idealism, and of the centrality of woman to herself are kept.

Each of the modern Lesbian poets under discussion proceeds with a very particular process of creating a new mythology. Valuing the bond of Lesbianism, speaking out from it into the modern world, we define origin or homeland as an ideal place. Then, by ferrying the modern world into that poetry with us, we place the most extreme and stereotyped women's powers of our experience into the exact center of the modern world, infusing them not only with value and history, but with centrality and finally with god-head, immanence, to use Starhawk's word, and godmind.

The effect of exchange is uncanny, is transformational. For the procedure produces, or induces, an *inversion*, as though one reached down a coat sleeve and pulled at the sleeve tip, tugging until it reversed, revealing an entirely different pattern and meaning of the coat than the one formerly exposed.

When Adrienne Rich places women in history and Jewish women (as she has done in *Sources*) in the central position of the universe of her poetry, she produces, or induces, from the Chosen People, a new and vibrant *choosing woman*. A woman of choices who takes full responsibility for her choices even when, as in "Phantasia for Elvira Shatayev," they lead to her certain death on a mountain-climbing expedition. The consequence of taking responsibility for making choices is that she also takes full responsibility for her powers, for locating and using them. The woman of Rich's poetry emerges out of history as more-than-history, more than singled-out, she becomes selector and judge as well. She is connected to all the natural universe; no longer walking a linear time path only, she can see beyond time. She is no longer split away from the universe, she is integrated with it.

When Parker spoke of place, it was her will operating: "I have placed this body, placed this mind" . . . in dreams of Malcolm X, Martin Luther King, Angela Davis. "Now you listen!" the poet demands, "I have a dream too . . . a simple dream" that wherever she goes, all her selves can go with her. This is not simple, it's actually revolutionary, a place in motion.

When Olga Broumas places the women of Western traditional myth into sexual relation to each other, explicit and detailed, the formerly degraded mythic sexual being of the woman becomes exalted. She is sacred and at the same time tremendously real and present, *god in the flesh*, wet, trembling, alive and right there beside you, inside you, all over your life, sharp and warm and painful and demanding and passionate and sacred.

When Audre Lorde takes the traditional American myth that has sealed Blackness in with terror and violence, has tarred and feathered it with threat and supernatural physical powers, when she takes this flint-black cutting edge of all our nightmares into the exact center of the universe of her work, giving the woman all the dimensions of her form, charged with her erotic sensibility of Lesbianism, the result is transformative. The woman who emerges from the boiling pit of racist, misogynist, alienating, and very industrial America is a warrior who combines anger with love, not conquest, not slaughter, not self-destruction, but anger with love, two-in-one, a "colossa," a very special kind of woman warrior who comes from the ideal place of Dan. As such she is a protector, a mother-warrior who has undertaken to use her tongue as a sword, with capacity to slice away the sludge and dross, to warm what is alive and to kill meticulously "what is already dead," leaving a freshly shining place, a surface of "black light." She is a warrior who is protector rather than conqueror. She is also the "destructor" as creator, the anger that prepares a new path. She is the creator who is herself in danger of destruction and who in protecting herself creates protection for others. In this process of inverting the myth of race in America, "Blackness and whiteness," the terror and violence in each of us can resolve into anger, be integrated into our lives and allowed to co-exist with love.

In my work the "common" and the highly charged folk underground of European Gay and female-based tribal cultural values are catapulted into a central position that places power directly into the hands of women, locates it there, who have had it torturously usurped as long ago as ten centuries or far more. Pervasive passivity is over-turned by this return to recognition and centrality of the ancient powers; the woman who emerges from the definition of a life that has been mute, battered and like a pale shadow, comes out with courage and joy. The poems call on her to bestir her memory, her mysticism, and her claim to powers.

The poems say that this is done simply by willful effort, by the creative force of "work," by resolve and intent, and by staying on this earth, in this life and in touch with facts rather than attempting to escape or deny. What had been seen as common, a dull drudgery, is now seen as beautiful. This is not alienated beauty, a toy or a sterile weapon of whiteness dragged from colonial era to colonial era. This is ripe, rich beauty as it is in the universe, the beauty of love as it manifests in the burning and cooling stars that become planets on purpose, as well as butterflies that be-come worms on purpose, becomes the substance and rela-tionship of the intelligent, forceful esthetic that is all life.

In Paula Gunn Allen's work, placement of the Ameri-can Indian as a woman in the central position completely alters the patriarchal belief that the Indian people were marauding horse-riders living on the fringe of "civi-lized" society. Allen's work pulls this false idea away like the flimsy justifying curtain that it is, revealing the tribal mother who is actually there. We see, rather than exoticized relics, the woman (the Indigenous people, the originators) who is the central provider of so much of our wealth, our health, and our knowledge of freedom and rights of the individual. The American dream itself lies behind the curtain Allen pulls off for us. The woman who is there is the source; she is the underlying network that sustains all the superstructure of industrial life. Nor will the things we value and neglect to value, the live earth, the good food, healing herbs, and great continental spaciousness, the crisp, clean air, lovely fierce animals, and the essential individual freedoms—nor will they survive our neglect if we neglect and destroy the people who produced and respected them. By recognizing and re-valuing the gynarchic and essentially woman-bonded matrix underlying what we say we treasure, we may yet realize the golden possibility; we may all even see that we, too, came from and can reconstruct such worlds.

Returning to Sappho's Gods

And now, having gone through some history and speculation, description and revelation, it seems appropriate to look once more at Sappho's use of the gods in her work and in her world.

Suppose that in part at least, what the ancients named as gods were highly developed psychic states ("the sleep of enchantment"[29]) achieved through using clear emotions: Aries, anger; Aphrodite, love; Adonis, tragic sorrow. Suppose that, when Sappho said that Aphrodite lives in a golden house, she was describing the way love looks inside ourselves, when we are able to enter the psychic mode of seeing/feeling, as she was. And we know that along with the destruction of Sappho's work from the ancient world, there has also been suppression of the psychic plane (until recently) and of the erotic dimension of the sacred. The psychic world, incidentally, is accessed most successfully by people who are firmly, even grossly, in contact with their own physicality.

As I have described in detail in *Another Mother Tongue* (in "Friction Among Women"), on occasion while making love with my lover, Paula Gunn Allen, I have experienced love as "a golden glow." Within the visual sensation we two call "psychic sex," we've been able to transmit images from one mind to the other and enhance our own visions. This ability spills into our lives in general, enabling us, at times, to "talk" to each other over long distance.

Audre Lorde in her essay "Uses of the Erotic: The Erotic as Power" discusses at length the all-pervasive importance of recognizing and allowing the powers of the erotic to permeate every facet of our lives. She suggests the erotic as a golden color in an image of the yellow powder used briefly after World War II to give white margarine a butter color.[30]

If I myself have seen love on the psychic plane, seen/ felt it as a brilliant yellow light that allowed me to speak to my lover though she was five hundred, or three thousand, miles away—surely the great Sappho saw it also, saw it tenfold more clearly, born as she was into a culture that had named the very quality of Psyche herself. And H.D. saying of the goddess she saw, and that she wore a colorless seamless gown, predicted that the goddess would return as Psyche, the butterfly. H.D. also predicted that in the future artists would appear who could access the "overmind," or "love-mind," as she described it in *Notes on Thought and Vision*.

Suppose Sappho was describing having access to the godforce of Aphrodite on the psychic plane, through the medium of sexual and emotional love, visualized as a golden light, a golden nectar poured into a golden cup, a golden house, a golden throne on which the god sat, the vehicle by which she arrived into Sappho's mind. Suppose Sappho was describing the sound that accompanied this vision from the astral plane, as a whirring like sparrows' wings.

In the most matter-of-fact imaginable way, as is appropriate in approaching those on the other side, in the higher mind, as it is sometimes called, Sappho asked Aphrodite for a favor:

> Ornate-throned immortal Aphrodite, wile-weaving daughter of Zeus, I entreat you: do not overpower my heart, mistress, with ache and anguish, but come here, if ever in the past you heard my voice from afar and acquiesced and came, leaving your father's golden house, with chariot yoked: beautiful swift sparrows whirring fast-beating wings brought you above the dark earth down from heaven through the mid-air, and soon they arrived; and you, blessed one, with a smile on your immortal face asked what was the matter with me this time and what in my maddened heart I most wished to happen for myself: 'Whom am I to persuade this time to lead you back to her lover? Who wrongs you, Sappho? If she runs away, soon she shall pursue; if she does not accept gifts, why, she shall give them instead; and if she does not love, soon she shall love even against her will.' Come to me now again and deliver me from oppressive anxieties; fulfil all that my heart longs to fulfil, and you yourself be my fellowfighter. (Greek Lyric, 53–54)

These are perfectly clear instructions to a god who approaches on the psychic plane, flowing down through the mid-air, from a golden house, manifesting with a smile, entreated directly and simply to do a certain favor. The words have the ring of the voices of teachers and spirit-guides heard in modern psychic readings: lovely, spare, descriptive, and to the point.[31]

In another fragment Sappho says that Love came down from heaven wearing a purple mantle. Suppose this is a description of a similar sort: that, caught deep in the emotion of love, she called on a god of the psychic dimension and was visited with a visualization of intense color, purple. Or perhaps she spotted a purple aura just outside Aphrodite's normal golden one. Or perhaps the aura was that of one of her lovers, was Love wearing a purple mantle.

Perhaps we are closer to recovering large portions of Sappho's world than we realize. By integrating our fragmented selves, and by subverting and dissembling the patriarchal order and worldview, we work to create a new paradigm, a new thought from Thought Woman's weaving basket, a new dream, a new web, a common language hitherto forgotten or suppressed, a common mind, a new possibility for recovering our highest apple: the special uses of love, beauty, and intelligence with which it is possible to live lives of justice, grace, and meaning.

If there are Lesbian deities with whom we are in dialogue, from our current "maddened hearts," what now do we ask of them?

RESPONSES

LESBiAN TiME
Donika Kelly

In Judy Grahn's *The Highest Apple*, lesbian time un-folds—geologic—around me, activates me as a fault line is activated. Something shifts. Tectonic. A tumble of recognition. Here is the island and the garden and the house of women. Here is lineage and genealogy and comfort to see myself in the long line of lesbian poets.

I am reading *The Highest Apple* on unceded, occupied territory—on an island not my own, O'ahu. The volcano is long silent. I am adrift—loosed, for a time—from the notion of home. I have come here to think about the humpbacks that spend November to April calving, mating, and, in my observation, frolicking in the waters surrounding the Hawaiian Islands. I am proximate to this part of their annual journey. Grahn invokes "woman as earth," recognizes "the earth as active principle," and alive as volcano, as stone, as living fruit (88). Who might breach the surface—as animal or new land—given the chance? Who might come to rest given enough time?

If "the white man's burden," Grahn writes, "is to be the center for everyone" in order to be perceived as universal, then the lesbian's gift is to embrace commonality, where common means "many-centered, many overlapping islands of groups each of which maintains its own center" (128). I get centered and consider empire. I get centered and consider family and migration. I get centered and consider the brittling bonds of biological kinship, consider reciprocal altruism—how briefly humpbacks might pair up to mate or feed or travel alongside one another. How queer it all seems, this bonding beyond blood.

Grahn welcomes me, common and whole, into the house of women, connected to a group, to a time, to a "universe that has a place for us" (50-51). The house of women, where the ordinary lives of women are made central, where wholeness and integration of the self is priority—this house cracks the foundational Western myth of patriarchy by decentering cisgender men and the patriarchy. How many houses now? How many islands?

And what to make of the gods? There are Sappho's, of course, but also the gods of Emily Dickinson, Adrienne Rich, Audre Lorde, Paula Gunn Allen, Olga Broumas, and even Grahn herself. I have laid to rest my old gods, halted the search for new ones and for old hierarchy. Can we engage with mythic time without hierarchy? How can we imagine connection that does not depend on myths of dominion? Grahn imagines, through praxis, connection without dominion. She calls us into the history of lesbian poetry; calls us ordinary; calls us common; shows us shared metaphors; shows us around the house; invites us to eat, to drink, to come to know one another.

In The Highest Apple, I locate a root of my own practice. I look across my body of work, which is one body among many. I made the island inland. Made it so I could carry it anywhere. Carried the island from high desert to timberlands to the central valley to the top of the Appalachian plateau. Carried my island to Brooklyn, then to the prairie. The island: what remains after exile from the father, the mother's death and resurrection, the marriage and the marriage's end. The island: a garden tended by women; the tending itself a bumper crop. The island anchored in an archipelago.

Donika Kelly is the author of *The Renunciations* and *Bestiary*. A recipient of a fellowship from the National Endowment for the Arts, she is a Cave Canem graduate fellow and founding member of the collective Poets at the End of the World. She currently lives in Iowa City, where she teaches creative writing the University of Iowa.

ASSEMBLiNG THE PiECES
Kim Shuck

It's really hard for me to write a response to anything by Judy Grahn without seeming like a fan girl. There is no way for me to look back at my baby writer self and see any path to where I am now without Grahn's essential works on being a woman, writing as a woman, and understanding literary canon as a woman. I take this literary lineage personally because I have made parts of my owned self from Grahn's words. It is because of Grahn and others like her that I did not have to come awake as a poet to find that I'd been entirely written out of possibility. I may be stitching on this collective quilt, but I didn't have to imagine it for myself and I will always be grateful for that.

When I first read *The Highest Apple*, the literature classes I was taking often treated women writers as oddities, individuals, not part of a literary history or continuum. Things had begun to shift—my high school poetry class included work by Adrienne Rich, but there was no sense of her as part of any community in particular. In fact, I wrote a paper about her and my English teacher said that she was happy I had because: "you seem to have a sympathy for that lifestyle." I have to confess that I was no good at coded language and assumed that she meant that I was a poet, and not that she was alluding to school rumors that my best friend and I were lovers. In fact, books like *The Highest Apple* gave me a place to exist. With a publishing date in the mid-1980s, it came after I'd graduated high school, but I clearly remember the deep, relaxing, breath of air that it afforded me.

Grahn describes a sense of particles of information coming together: the work of Sappho, information from writers like Paula Gunn Allen and Pat Parker. I remember it being exactly as she describes: pieces coming together. In the case of Sappho, pieces are all that we have. In the case of Emily Dickinson, the pieces were all there, but it was still very difficult to contextualize her. Her writing was viewed as important, but her self, the way that she found voice, her identity as anything other than just strange, was not generally investigated. In the sense that there was such a place as "that lifestyle," we were not offered a Dickinson who existed there.

My first books about women's culture were purchased at occult stores. It seems baffling looking back on it. The idea of a women's spirituality was, even in wild old San Francisco, pretty marginal. Then it wasn't. The work of Grahn herself—and Luisah Teish, and Allen, and others mentioned in *The Highest Apple*—was in large part responsible for that shift.

The Highest Apple was written during a time when erased, forgotten, and carefully hidden things were being reclaimed. It's an important piece to visit today as a map of that process. Today, in the 2020s, the United States is enduring another struggle of awareness. Denial, lies, erasures: tracking a true path is as difficult now as it ever has been; awareness is a practice, and not an easy one. This book is not just a great book to read for the information it offers; it's not just great as a historical piece from the last century; it's not just a fun reminiscence for those of us who were there and then—it's a very honest book that tracks some of what it is to make space for a denied tradition. We need that now as we did then, and we probably will in the future.

Kim Shuck writes many small autobiographies. Here in October, Shuck is mostly fair to partly cloudy with the possibility of cookie baking at any moment. Shuck served as the seventh Poet Laureate of San Francisco beginning in 2017. Kim's most recent publications include a collection of poems called Exile Heart, a collection of essays called Noodle, Rant, Tangent, and three efforts in editing including a small anthology of San Francisco poets. Kim needs a nap.

A HOUSE OF HAUNTED WOMEN
Serena Chopra

Perhaps, like me, other millennial lesbians reading
Grahn's *The Highest Apple* will feel haunted by the
ways the text nagged the fraught seams negotiating Les-
bian Feminism, Transfeminism, Transnational Femi-
nism, Queer Theory, and other contemporary queer and
radical sociopolitical perspectives. Despite attempting a
contemporary intersectional approach, Grahn's text of-
ten lacks attention to the implications of difference—and,
as a Punjabi-American lesbian poet, I found myself navi-
gating a distressed relationship with the text, one that
echoed my childhood on the predominantly white Ameri-
can Great Plains of the 1980s. My experiences growing up
there and then were characterized equally by invisibility,[1]
an (enforced? persuaded? expected?) appreciation for
representation (despite it being blurry and inept), and the
confusing sorrow of acceptance, all manifested by Ameri-
can "melting-pot" ethics that worked to erase difference.
For me, this was particularly present in the clumping of
all brown bodies as the ethnically ambiguous token, the
not-white-but-not-Black doll of cultural capital.

I applaud the boldness of the text in its historical con-
text and recognize the immense importance of its work—
proclaiming, legitimizing, and articulating the personal,
political, and poetic significance of centering lesbians

in an effort to shift away from the patriarchy-centered, heteronormative-aligned, "male-identified"[2] politics of inclusion[3] sought by Grahn's straight feminist contemporaries, and toward the "many-centered" islands of "woman-identified," autonomously empowered community and consciousness sought by the Radicalesbians. Simultaneously, I was perturbed by the deep wounds of our myopic lesbian histories, especially those that, in an effort to fix all women as "common" ("to concretize the bonding of women into a group identity" [129]), erased significant tensions of difference. First, the prevailing second-wave concept of universal "sisterhood" fettered "woman" to mythic (mostly Western) conceptions of "female" anatomy, thereby sustaining the privileged, exclusionary, and violent effects of gender fatalism—including stud-, butch-, and transphobia—and, in effect, reinforcing the violence of the "male/female myth" that Grahn's "bonding of women" claims to escape. Second, I understand that Grahn is working with a notion of commonality that embraces centering the many islands of race and class difference, "each of which maintains its own center and each of which is central to society for what it gives to society," imagining, too, that we can "[retain] racial and ethnic identities without losing either our affinity as women and or as Lesbians," that we can, for example, exist as both lesbian and Punjabi-American (132). But this has not always been possible or true for me. Grahn's argument assumes that there is equal power among women to know of, feel legitimized by, dedicate themselves as, and connect to a "common" mythic past that will lead us toward a future lesbian civitas organized under a metaethics of *wholeness* (225) that is ultimately imagined from an American history, culture, and education. The ways in which this logic allows whiteness, Americanness, and a Western tailoring of mythology to wholly assume and subsume Otherness feels as desperate, didactic, and awkward as the bright diversity mural I painted in second grade (and again in fourth and eighth and tenth) alongside my white teachers and schoolmates—the gaudiness of white guilt, its brash representations (blurry and inept) of inclusion that tokenize and assimilate through a showy evasion of ongoing systemic violences. Though Grahn keenly attends to decentering whiteness from lesbianism, the book does not dislodge lesbianism from whiteness. Grahn's alignment of Sappho's House of Women, Lowell's garden, Dickinson's heaven, and H.D.'s white isle (158) as the place of lesbian wholeness is inevitably the construction of a white American imaginary. Though the *diverse faces of poetry* are represented, the link between wholeness and whiteness in America cannot be ignored—I could not ignore it, it has always shattered me at the core. Additionally, the desire to be located, to have place—especially in its relationship to home/house—is steeped in violent histories of gender fatalism. Thus, the desire to be in the House of Women is a desire to be whole, to be "female," to be like-white. Ultimately, it is Grahn's metaethics of *wholeness* that most profoundly disturbs me in its kinship with whiteness, Western hermeneutics, and cisness. Plainly, I don't believe in it, I don't trust it.

So, what good does it do to republish *The Highest Apple*? What is the import and impact of a dated queer text on an audience thirty-eight years after its original publication, for 2023 and beyond? Despite my critiques, how is it that Grahn's incisive and embodied scholarship lingers in my nervous system—what is this lingering—and why does it move me—I'll admit it—to tears? Despite the validity of my critiques, the gorgeous and poignant constellation Grahn has crafted between historical lesbian poets and her contemporary community of lesbian poets shoots like a magnetic star through my own experiences, gathering debris into a cosmos of lesbian desire. In this cosmos, Grahn asks me to witness in the galactic eyes of our Sapphic mothers a historical vision of myself as desire, as future. In her attention to the nuanced and psychic lesbian wisdom of desire—of reaching—I face a lineage: the forces calibrating our contemporary vision, those forces desiring before Sappho and after (forever after her), incanting lesbian possibility to rise and rise (the apples higher each season)—and I am infinitely humbled by the act of poetry to labor, love, and will desire into language, into being.

Predating but akin to José Muñoz's conception of the "queer horizon," Grahn's ecstatic remembering of lesbian pasts illuminates and overflows her present with ecstatic potential for queer living and loving—the highest apple is indeed "a place of the past that is actually waiting for us in the future" (84). Grahn's text does not merely evidence lesbians (she, like us, knows we've existed—we must have existed—because desire reaches backward, too). Rather, she engages lesbian poets as mediums, as psychic recorders of how queer desire transforms and reimagines all of society (for example, as "many-centered," and as refusing victimization by being erotically attuned[4]) by decentering patriarchal structures (exemplified, for instance, in Stein's destabilization of masculine discourse and H.D.'s re-vision of the previously male-dominated epic form). In attending to the ephemeral debris of lesbian poetry—that which is sought and collected by future lesbian readers—Grahn's constellating study illuminates the "many-centered" force of both queerness and poetry, propelling her to imagine the ways each might eventually inspire a sustained decentering of whiteness. Like poetry, queerness revels in impossible possibilities, in discovering the impossible as possible—alighting a dark room with the glittering angles of kinetic potential and startling desire into sound, into forms, into further reaching: for resonance, resonant forms and nervous systems, nervous systems and bodies, bodies many-minded and multiplying. And the inherent queerness of poetry compels emergence—poetry recording the ephemera of desire and becoming, bringing what is just out of reach into vision, into a language, a sensation, a communion, a potential illuminating psychic shapes in the stars of our gathering.

It is Grahn's meaningful, cross-temporal arrangements and alignments that implore us to open a place for *The Highest Apple* as a cultural site within our queer present. In "Haunted by Her: Lesbian Feminist Ghostly Drags on Representation and Reception," lesbian artist Allyson Mitchell speaks on the "ghost[s] of lesbian politics"—those radical lesbian feminist histories that continue to haunt our contemporary radical perspectives, approaches, and work. While I agree with Mitchell's gesture toward "archiv[ing] the loss of cultural sites and let[ting] them go for a future that is unknown," I am also inspired—in some cases—to unearth and re-member cultural sites that, though a bit crude and incomplete, have meaningfully contributed to queer becoming and which also exemplify possibilities for making unknown queer futures more possible. Grahn herself notes the discrepancy in her constellation, recognizing that "Sappho's work indicated none of the restrictions, lack of safety, fear of reprisal by husband, police, or other patriarchal institution. Her world was not patriarchal." Therefore, in a gesture that by no means forgives the troubling Lesbian feminist ghosts that haunt Grahn's book, but also feeling dissatisfied by putting them to rest—I desire to use them as tensions. This is to say that I believe in collective wisdom, and I am interested in using it to construct a tensegral shelter/structure/place for lesbian desire.

A tensegral structure is supported by tensions, which utilize traction and compression between taut cables and rigid poles to delineate the structure's space. Imitating natural biological structures (such as the relationship between muscle and bone), a tensegral shelter is stabilized by rods that bear the load (compression) of the tension created by the oppositional pull (traction) of the cables between them. To reach for the highest apple, one must relevé, pushing their toes into the ground—hand and foot stretching in opposition, muscles in traction, balanced and stabilized by the compression held in the bones.

One of the best qualities of tensegrity, as articulated by R. Buckminster Fuller, is that since none of the beams (islands, stars, eras) touch (being held instead by tension), there is no limit to the amount of tension that the structure can bear, allowing it to enclose unlimited space (his example is the gravitational tension between the Earth and the moon). Not only am I interested in describing tensegrity as a place for lesbian futurities—believing that diverse wisdoms-in-tension (such as how both coming out/visibility and staying in/invisibility have been powerful strategies for lesbian possibility) will sustain us—but

I also recognize (like Grahn) that the cultural sites of lesbian pasts often lend themselves to tensegral hermeneutical approaches; for example, reading as a reshaping of the myths constellated by the ghosts of lesbian politics.

My reshaping of Grahn's text proposes that Grahn's cross-temporality opposes her argument for the recovery of wholeness. Secondary to a metaethics of wholeness, Grahn's approach to centering lesbians involves reordering the patriarchal hierarchy of gender. Her revision of "the usual patriarchal myth of feminine/masculine class structure" (162) aims to create a new mythology that is "an inversion, as though one reached down a coat sleeve and pulled at the sleeve tip, tugging until it reversed" (225-226). This inversion, however, draws me to consider French feminist and lesbian Luce Irigaray's warning in *This Sex Which is Not One*: "But if [woman's] aim were simply to reverse the order of things, even supposing this to be possible, history would repeat itself in the long run, would revert to sameness: to phallocratism. It would leave room neither for women's sexuality, nor for women's imaginary, nor for women's language to take (their) place" (33). Where Grahn claims inversion "of the patriarchal order and worldview" as a tactic for "recovering our highest apple," I suggest a reshaping of her conception as one that is *rhizomic* rather than inverting and is *reaching* rather than recovering. As exemplified by fungi and aspen trees, rhizomes are subterranean, horizontally spreading and vertically shooting root structures. Rhizomes reach from their eyes, each eye a node of possibility seeing through dark earth, sending shoots toward the sun. Rhizomes, like tensegrity, illustrate decentralized visionary modalities that rely on multiple intelligences and experiences held in tension (traction-compression; vertical-horizontal)—and Grahn helps us see "women's imaginary" as a place holding/held in its spreading and simultaneously reaching, reaching.

Rather than reversing the sleeve of patriarchy to assert "the gynarchic and essentially woman-bonded matrix," *The Highest Apple* reveals place as a decentralized network of kinship and ecstatic temporality.[5] Though Grahn often forces the content of the poetry (including the poets' race and spiritual backgrounds) into discomforting equalizations in an effort to prove wholeness, the greater conceptual gestures of her book inspire an ecstatic cross-temporal re-membering, moving us out of the hetero-dominant present[6] and into a "many-centered," multivalent, and resonant "psychic rebirth" of woman and society through lesbian poetry, the tensegral place of "women's imaginary." The result is an expansive performance that decenters the singular, linear intelligence of hetero-patriarchal capital order in favor of multiple queer intelligences and embodied experiences, thereby resembling a rhizome's subterranean spread and vertical shoot—or, figuratively, subversive desire and becoming, the impossible made possible. In reshaping Grahn's recovery of wholeness as *rhizomic reach*, it becomes clear that she is an early proponent for theorizing how "multiple forms of belonging in difference adhere to a belonging in collectivity" (Muñoz, 20).

Grahn reaches through time, alighting a dark room with the glittering angles of kinetic potential, opening room for lesbian poetry "to take [its] place"—"a place where the usual strident, linear oppositions no longer prevail because we shall have made a larger metaphor that incorporates the oppositional one within it" (224). And, in a final reshaping of Grahn's conception, place—though rooted in placenta—grows deeper than anatomy; place keeps losing the metaphor and exceeds the integration of opposites; place discharges beyond the "lochial blood" of being fixed by the location of categorical belonging (beyond, for example, the fixed category of "woman" that assumes all AFAB (assigned female at birth) folks connect to the mythic female womb and that no other genders possibly could). Encountering The Highest Apple as "a place of the past that is actually waiting for us in the future" (84), I desire to decenter Grahn's decentering of place, to go beyond only incorporating the oppositional and expanding to include the transitional, the flux, the lost, the unfixed, the disoriented, dislocated, and diasporic—queerness and all its potential. I desire a Tensegral House of Women, a place in tension with its ghosts. And I center lesbians, knowing that ghosts are being made always as we speak, read. What kind of lesbian ghosts will we be?

References

Buckminster Fuller on Tensegrity Structures - YouTube. https://www.youtube.com/watch?v=7JwOX4PlO2A.

Irigaray, Luce. This Sex Which Is Not One. Translated by Catherine Porter with Carolyn Burke. Ithaca: Cornell University Press, 1985.

Mitchell, Allyson. "Haunted by her: lesbian feminist ghostly drags on representation and reception." Feminist Theory vol. 20, no. 4 (2019): 431–43.

Muñoz, José Esteban. Cruising Utopia: The Then and There of Queer Futurity. New York: New York University Press, 2009.

Radicalesbians. "The Woman-Identified Woman." In *The Second Wave: A Reader in Feminist Theory*, edited by Linda Nicholson, 153–7. New York: Routledge, 1997.

Serena Chopra is a writer, dancer, filmmaker, a visual and performance artist, and a teacher. She has a PhD in Creative Writing from the University of Denver and is a MacDowell Fellow, a Kundiman Fellow and a Fulbright Scholar. She has two books and two films. Serena is Assistant Professor of Creative Writing at Seattle University. You can find out more at SerenaChopra.com

QUEER ELDERS GIVE US A PLACE TO ARRIVE

Zoe Tuck

In *Another Mother Tongue: Gay Words, Gay Worlds*, published in 1984 (the year of my birth and a year before the publication of *The Highest Apple*), Judy Grahn addresses her investigations into queer culture to her first lover, returning a gift that her lover gave to her by expanding on the lore and language of lesbianism at length. In the chapter "Sashay Down the Lavender Trail," Grahn writes:

> I thought that if Gayness has cultural characteristics, then it exists as a separate entity, complete in itself, and not as a reaction to a heterosexual social model, not as a reaction to any social model, including sexism, patriarchy, the way men or women are treated by each other, the fact that families stay together or split up, that sexuality is open or closed, that the economy is flourishing or depressed. If Gayness has a culture of its own, it exists in the midst of but is not caused by any of those conditions. (19)

As a young person, I didn't just dream of being recognized as a woman and a lesbian, I longed to participate in a queer culture that had only been present to me in books, although books that led me to the queer life I lead today and which continue to sustain me. I mention the coincidence that one of Grahn's books was published the year I was born as a way of recognizing that when I eventually found my way to queer culture, it is a culture that Grahn helped, and continues to help, build. Queer elders give us a place to arrive.

In *The Highest Apple*, as well as in previous works like *Another Mother Tongue* and later works like *Eruptions of Inanna*, Grahn delves into history and mythology for roots in the past, however hidden or suppressed. How do I view this as a place-making endeavor? Grahn writes:

> Having a mythic history with genuine godforces operating on a daily level is completely necessary to the Lesbian poetic search for what Mary Carruthers calls a new Lesbian *civitas*, a paradigm, a model of a new community, a new relationship of women to the world. (204)

We arrive to a culture, as much as to a society; and mythology is central to the transmission of culture. This powerful early realization of Grahn's prompts her to reach across cultures to find analogues and connections to the contemporary lesbian culture from which and to which she writes.

Grahn shares affinities with one of the first trans writers I found when I was a young closeted trans lesbian, searching the shelves of the local bookstore for some reflection of myself, some context other than lurid talk show depictions of trans women. Revolutionary socialist Leslie Feinberg's *Transgender Warriors* makes similar moves to Grahn in terms of a cross-cultural study of gender variance.

In some ways, the academic disciplines (Women's, Gender, and Sexuality Studies; Trans Studies) that are in conversation with similar topics have developed a resistance to this comparatist approach. In part, this resistance reflects a corrective to overzealous attempts to impose Eurocentric definitions of gender and sexuality across cultures. However, I believe that writers like Grahn and Feinberg have been drawn to a comparatist approach through their activism, which necessitates coalition-building—making common cause across (but not erasing) difference.

Grahn's literary works and public scholarship are continuous with her activism—and her spirituality. "Mythic realism" is her name for the continuity of approach that she finds in her peers and predecessors reaching back to Sappho and Enheduanna:

> We do not take the sacred, the political, the social, the details of everyday, and carry them "away" or split them from each other. We place them all together in the real lives of real women in the present, in the raucous, dangerous, tumultuous marketplace/urban/warzone/suburb of modern life. As Sappho did. In this way we can help to re-found a House of Women from which to approach all other worlds, reconnections to the Roses of the Muses, making more intact the fabric of Lesbian myth. (165)

The House of Women is multidimensional: it can be a physical space—a gay bar, a bookstore—but also a literary space or a relational one, a dream or a memory. I tried to get at this multidimensionality in a poem called "The Women's Building," in which musing about the eponymous mural-clad building in San Francisco leads me to meditate on what Grahn calls the House of Women as an ideal. I write:

> I want to go into the Women's Building. What happens inside the Women's Building? Is it where one becomes a woman, or perhaps where one might go to have their womanhood verified? Now there's a terrible thought: they'd probably ask for two forms of ID, a credit card, an insurance card; in the US we have this thing called a credit score. Maybe they'd even ask me for a letter from a psychologist, or my medical doctor, proof of surgery, things like that. Thing is, I'm on hormones, have been for years, but I've never had any kind of surgery. But maybe they wouldn't ask for any such thing, maybe those things are anathema to the ethos of the Women's Building.
>
> Anathema, ethos; phallogocentric. I think briefly of L. saying that she has intentionally de-skilled herself.
>
> Other ways of being "in" the Women's Building: being "in" a friendship between women; making love like women do with each other (a kind of mirroring, S. uses the word "twincest," shocking my delicate sensibilities); comfort with ambiguity; responsibility, right or wrong, for the recreation of the world.

I've always believed that being a woman, a woman who loves women, and a poet are, or ought to be, sacred. Living in a materialist culture fills me with doubt about this deeply held belief.

Fortunately, I can turn to Grahn's work, which demonstrates an ongoing commitment to recovering and creating spiritual technologies as part of the work of lesbian culture. This is powerfully present to me throughout *The Highest Apple*, but especially in the section "Returning to Sappho's Gods." Here, Grahn considers Sappho's gods as psychic states from which we have been alienated. But lesbian feminist spirituality does not cut out the body. Far from it! Grahn writes, "The psychic world, incidentally, is accessed most successfully by people who are firmly, even grossly, in contact with their own physicality" (230). And not just physicality but sensuality, eroticism. As Grahn writes in *Eruptions of Inanna*, "What was going on with intensely desired female beauty linked to shame and death? My writing life has been haunted by this theme" (139). To extend this question, I ask: What becomes possible when you uncouple female desire from shame and death? *The Highest Apple*, along with the rest of Grahn's oeuvre, stands in answer to this question, and generously invites readers in to live and write answers of our own.

References

Feinberg, Leslie. *Transgender Warriors: Making History from Joan of Arc to RuPaul.* Beacon Press, 1996.

Grahn, Judy. *Another Mother Tongue: Gay Words, Gay Worlds.* Beacon Press, 1984.

Grahn, Judy. *Eruptions of Inanna: Justice, Gender, and Erotic Power.* Nightboat Books & Sinister Wisdom, 2021.

Grahn, Judy. *The Highest Apple: Sappho and the Lesbian Poetic Tradition.* First edition, Spinsters, Ink, 1985.

Magloire, Aaron, Alma Valdez-García, James Loop, Paige Parsons, Rebecca Ramdhan, Zoe Tuck. *May No Emails Find You: Poems from the Belladonna* Studio.* Belladonna*, 2021.

Zoe Tuck was born in Texas, became a person in California, and lives in Western Massachusetts. She is the author of Bedroom Vowel (BUNNY Presse, 2023) and Terror Matrix (Timeless, Infinite Light, 2014), and the chapbooks The Book of Bella (Doublecross Press), bound with Emily Hunerwadel's Peach Woman, and Vape Cloud of Unknowing (Belladonna* Collaborative). With Britt Billmeyer-Finn, she co-hosts The But Also reading series and she co-edits Hot Pink Magazine with Emily Bark Brown.

MAPPING COMMUNITY AND/AS EXPRESSIONS OF LOVE

Saretta Morgan

This response to *The Highest Apple* opened very differently. Then, a few days ago I attended a wedding. A very small, queer Sonoran desert wedding. We caravanned after sunset to a corner of (non-reservation) Tohono O'odham land less than fifty miles north from the current US–Mexico border.

Surrounded by the scent of creosote, and with nothing visible but moonlit desert beyond the circle of our bonfire, the two lovers sat on the ground opposite each other enclosed by a sphere of chosen kin (both blood and not). As community around the lovers, we'd been invited to meditate, mostly in silence, over the course of an hour on our relationships to each other and to love. The fire crackled. Multiple coyotes howled and yipped nearby. Here and there, voices broke the silence to share what these two lovers had taught them about care, collectivity, joy, articulating desire, and the intentional structuring of life.

In one pocket of silence a thought rose in my mind: this is *what Grahn is doing*. Mapping community and/as expressions of love.

Grahn's practice of kinship is environmentally grounded, born through her attention to the many scales at which women's stories reflect, care for, and alter the world. Throughout The Highest Apple, Grahn reflects on lesbian relationships to land relative to self-actualization. Sappho opens the tradition in lush island landscapes. Audre Lorde's backyard garden transforms through lesbian union. Grahn's poetic protagonists assert themselves in parks and urban public spaces. Possibilities of becoming are offered in how lands are engaged, and in which bodies are made possible inside/alongside them.

I take pleasure in watching these women poets command their respective spaces. Hand-in-hand with that pleasure is my desire to see them burst every space at its seams. This desire, too, the text invites in a way. Grahn was inspired by Mary J. Carruthers's promise of "nothing less than the total transformation of our society,"[1] through the study and practice of Lesbianism as erotic criticality. Grahn further advanced that notion by bringing Indigenous sexuality clearly into the frame. In doing so she opened the door for a critique of lesbianism and sociality that it wasn't likely possible for a white woman in the '80s to develop. Not out of fear or lack of sense, but because Indigenous theorizing on sexuality relative to land had not been widely published in the United States at that time. Still, The Highest Apple moved closer to engaging the depth of awareness that social transformation requires.

Grahn was moved to include the work of Laguna Pueblo poet (and her then-lover) Paula Gunn Allen in order to allow an "American Indian voice [to complete] the picture of Lesbian presence on this American continent." Allen's work and life offer texture and context to conversations on land, sexuality, and female expression. Like Grahn, Allen deeply understood and published widely on male supremacy as the source of social and environmental destruction. She similarly held that without a restoration of feminine leadership, the earth as we know it will be short-lived. [2]

I read Grahn's incorporation of Allen into Carruthers's frame, and her movement toward a complete America, carefully. It's clear to me that Grahn isn't only speaking about the need for greater diversity (as the inclusion of one additional racial or ethnic minority would not constitute a "complete" reflection of America at that time). I believe Grahn was moved by an understanding that Indigenous knowledge systems bring something categorically different to the picture. And in the context of our settler-colonial US, that particular difference is fundamentally necessary to social transformation. We can't articulate and ethically mind the power that's exercised in how we relate to land as a physicality, and land as its practices of interfacing history and socio-ecological paradigms (of which poetry is one), on the soil this country inhabits without attention to Indigenous peoples.

I wonder, however, about the inclusion of Native knowledges without thorough attention to the terms under which those knowledges have become known to us. It rides a line of multiculturalism that assumes discrete bodies can aggregate into a perceivable whole, and further, that each body survives aggregation still whole. Generally speaking, these logics rely on practices of erasure that excise whatever fails to conform to the American value(s) of diversity. In this case, what is reiterated through Grahn's appreciation of Native women's contributions to lesbian poetry is that they offer a demonstrative longevity to her argument by "[giving] us our understanding of the world as a long, long story, which the four- or five-thousand-year rise and spread of the patriarchal form is only one aspect" (42). Native narratives do provide rich scales of time and experience, but when we draw on those knowledges without problematizing the context within which we encounter them (the context being occupation and forced internal displacement), our discourses of inclusion risk reproducing processes of assimilation. Assimilation is the agreement that one can exist so long as that existence doesn't disrupt a desired value. The value in this case, revolutionary lesbianism, suffers a de-prioritization of settler-colonial relations and the constant entanglement of those relations with gender in the US for all bodies, an absence that reconstitutes imaginative boundaries of sex and gender into alignment with the US State (and/as American continent) to erase Indigenous experience.

I'm not suggesting that for two or more women to have loving, open, sexual, intimate relationships among themselves constitutes a settler-colonial affair, but that to recognize those relationships within the history and understandings of "lesbian" as a default obscures other ways that bodies come to be known—through relationships to language, community, land—and the ways of life such knowings mutually rely on. Obfuscations of that order are what settler colonialism relies on to continue the dismantling of Indigenous cultures.

As I mentioned before, I don't believe that all the critiques possible to desire today were available in 1985. What's instructive to me is that Grahn knew we had somewhere to get. And she took a step. I honor every decision to shift the frame. There are no small ones, even when (and perhaps because) we aren't equipped to recognize all that one step brings into view. A sustained engagement with the fullness of Indigenous women and sexuality in the physical and literary landscapes of the United States insists that we deeply question and radically reconsider our relationships to this land, and to each other while we're standing on it.

What shifts into view when we take Allen's work as an Indigenous *intervention* as opposed to an Indigenous *extension* to the landscape of lesbian poetry in America? I believe the framework for making these inquiries is laid before us in *The Highest Apple* through the ways Grahn braids poetics, desire, and—importantly—the material conditions of life across the poets held in her gaze. As inheritors of Grahn's we can continue actualizing the potential in her gesture and the power of her formal approach to bring Indigenous experiences into a constellation dominated by Euro-American lesbian desire.

As the disruption of tribally specific practices of gender and sexuality through sexualized violence, boarding school systems, and forced and coercive transformations of political and domestic life underwrite the United States' ongoing occupation of Indigenous lands, interrogations of gender and indigeneity necessarily challenge settler colonialism. "Decolonization," writes Diné scholar Jennifer Denetdale, "necessarily employs gender as a category of analysis if Indigenous nations are ever to return to their own traditional principles as their foundation."[4] Because our complete American continent represents the continued dismantling of Indigenous sovereignty, which has always included unique practices of gender and sexuality, a complete American continent is physically and conceptually incompatible with the proliferation of sexually self-actualized tribal nations and peoples.

Concurrent to Grahn's publication of *The Highest Apple* in 1985, Indigenous peoples were drawing Allen into their own development of language for the connections between land, spirituality, and gender—a "sovereign erotic," which Indigenous Studies scholar Qwo-Li Driskill describes as the "return to and/or continuance of the complex realities of gender and sexuality that are ever present in both the human and more-than-human world but erased or hidden by colonial cultures." [5] Indigenous reclamation and re-imaginings of gender are decolonial practices. One highly visible manifestation of these conversations was the emergence of "Two-Spirit" in the 1980s as a term and analytic for wrestling the indivisibility of sexuality and indigeneity (Driskill), and for moving beyond the boundaries of US queer literature / US queer theory in which the settler state continues to persist as a self-obscuring baseline.

When Allen's novel *The Woman Who Owned the Shadows* appears in *The Highest Apple*, Grahn does acknowledge the role of boarding schools in removing Indigenous girls from their culture, but what she highlights of the novel is the punishment of two (white) nuns, who are separated after a joyous display of public affection. Grahn recognizes that boarding schools played a role in protecting the values of the state, but her gender analysis of what threatens those values stopped at the freedom of women to express authentic feelings in public. In this way, *The Woman Who Owned the Shadows* is able to support Grahn's objective in *The Highest Apple* to tend the "re-emergence of the public Lesbian voice," but unintentionally leans away from a deeply significant process of erasure with respect to Indigenous sexuality (36). Removing Indigenous children from their cultures was an attack on gender and sexuality at national/tribal and individual scales, one that won't be rectified through the public expression of lesbian values.

Allen's work was central to the development of Queer Native literary criticism, and responses to *The Woman Who Owned the Shadows* are foundational to Two-Spirit literary studies. "Reaction to [Allen's] creative and critical writing offers a window into the development of the field itself," wrote Lisa Tatonetti in "Indigenous Fantasies of Soverign Erotics."[6] It's a field of knowledge that Euro-American literary discourses attempt to dismantle and elide. US mainstream references to Two-Spirit often, and erroneously, imply that it's a kind of "trans identity for Native peoples." Consider for example that Two-Spirit poet Joshua Whitehead (Cree, Oji-Cree) was shortlisted for the 2018 Lambda Literary Award for Trans Poetry—a nomination the poet politely and politically declined, stating that they "recognize the difficulty of categorizing Two-Spirit (2SQ) within Western conceptualizations of sex, sexuality, and gender." Whitehead continued, stating, "I cling to Two-Spirit because it became an honour song that sung me back into myself as an Indigenous person, a nehiyaw (Cree), an Oji-Cree."[7] Whitehead is also clear that they are not speaking for all queer and nonbinary Indigenous peoples by personally distancing from the term "trans." The point isn't that some Indigenous people do or don't identify as LGBTQ, it's that the one-for-one equivocation of sexuality across settler-colonial lines strips Indigenous practices of their histories and political relevance.

Though Allen didn't identify as a Two-Spirit person, she was very clear that just as Native Americans "have never fit the descriptions other Americans imposed and impose, neither does [their] thought fit the categories that have been devised to organize Western intellectual enterprise." Allen illustrates practices of land that are spiritually and socially constituted by, she says, the "peculiarity of Native American life." She saw her work within the context of Native philosophy and to further "a Native turn of mind rather than Western inclination."[8]

Grahn shares a similar commitment to context. Adjacent with Paula Gunn Allen's fundamental question, "Who is your mother?"[9] Grahn models a practice—a devotion, even—of mapping community. Her sharpness as a poet, researcher, close-reader, theorist, and critic integrate to produce a literary structure that grounds each poet in the specificity of her own socio-geographic conditions, while linking them across social fabrics and time through the resonance and discord found in their language and emotional lives. The Highest Apple offers several histories as well as a very intentional practice of relation between women across class, space, and time. I think the deeper we engage this practice, the more able we are to expose the boundaries that reinscribe perceived separations of nation, sexuality, and gender.

Notes

1 In the first edition of The Highest Apple (1985), Grahn suggests that an analysis of white, Black, and Indigenous lesbian poets completes the context of American lesbian poetry: "From these interesting definitions, I drew some

criteria of my own with which to formulate the ideas I have set forth in *The Highest Apple*. The contemporary poets whose work I have chosen to discuss include all four of the ones included in Mary Carruthers's analysis, plus the inimitable Pat Parker with her direct critique of American society from a Black as well as a feminist perspective, and Paula Gunn Allen, whose Laguna Pueblo voice adds *critical dimension to the picture of Lesbian presence on this American continent*" (emphasis mine) (35).

6 "If we are male-identified in our heads, we cannot realize our autonomy as human beings" ("The Woman-Identified Woman" by the Radicalesbians, 1970).

5 "Insofar as women want only more privileges within the system, they do not want to antagonize male power. They instead seek acceptability for women's liberation, and the most crucial aspect of the acceptability is to deny lesbianism" ("The Woman-Identified Woman" by the Radicalesbians, 1970).

4 Aligning with Audre Lorde's thinking in "The Uses of the Erotic: The Erotic as Power" (1978).

3 "To see queerness as horizon is to perceive it as a modality of ecstatic time in which the temporal stranglehold that I describe as straight time is interrupted or stepped out of. Ecstatic time is signaled at the moment one feels ecstasy, announced perhaps in a scream or grunt of pleasure, and more importantly during moments of contemplation when one looks back at a scene from one's past, present, or future" (Muñoz, 32).

2 Referred to by Muñoz as the "here and now" of straight time which includes its capitally-enforced reproductions of heteronormativity: "Straight time tells us that there is no future but the here and now of our everyday life. The only futurity promised is that of reproductive majoritarian heterosexuality, the spectacle of the

state refurbishing its ranks through overt and subsidized acts of reproduction" (Muñoz, 22).

References

Mary J. Carruthers, "The Re-Vision of the Muse: Adrienne Rich, Audre Lorde, Judy Grahn and Olga Broumas," *Hudson Review* vol. 36 (1983).

Paula Gunn Allen, "The Anima of the Sacred: Empowering Women's Sexuality," *Off the Reservation* (Beacon Press, 1998).

Jennifer Denetdale, "Return to 'The Uprising at Beautiful Mountain in 1913,'" *Critically Sovereign* (Duke University Press, 2017).

Qwo-Li Driskill, "Stolen from Our Bodies: First Nations Two-Spirits/Queers and the Journey to a Sovereign Erotic," *Studies in American Indian Literature* 16, no. 2 (2004).

Lisa Tatonetti, "Indigenous Fantasies and Sovereign Erotics: Outland Cherokees Write Two-Spirit Nations," *Sovereign Erotics* (University of Arizona, 2011).

Joshua Whitehead, "Why I'm Withdrawing from My Lambda Literary Award Nomination," The Insurgent Architects blog, March 14, 2018, tiahouse.ca.

Allen, "Don't Fence Me In," *Off the Reservation*.

Saretta Morgan is the author of Alt-Nature (forthcoming from Coffee House Press, 2024), and the chapbooks Feeling Upon Arrival and room for a counter interior. Her work engages the emotional landscapes and languages of intimacy that manifest in the wake of militarization, incarceration, and U.S. imperialism. Learn more at www.sarettamorgan.com.

JUDY, NTOZAKE, COMMUNITY, AND POETRY

Khadijah Queen

This story begins on an elevator in Newark, New Jersey. Going down, from my tenth-floor room to the lobby of a high-rise hotel I can't remember the name of. A tall woman with a cloud of black curls wheeled another woman through the doors and I froze. The regally seated woman, with rainbow-colored yarn braided through her long hair, was Ntozake Shange. The shock of her presence stilled me. What do you say to a living legend? Surely not a plain hello. Rather than misspeak, I remained quiet, keeping all the wows and holyshitthatisNtozakeShanges to myself, letting them rapid-fire accumulate as energy (excitement? Panic? Awe? Nervousness?) in my tenderest interior—the one that discovered Shange's work at age fourteen and changed forever. That nervousness is funny because I'd been around celebrities my entire life, growing up and coming of age in Los Angeles, but around writers I admired—I did not know how to act.

Then I remembered I would see her later, since we were both on a panel called "Silence Is Become Speech," about women's voices in poetry, and I tried to breathe myself into some expression of calm. But by then, the lift bell dinged and its doors closed behind her.

Ntozake Shange performed at the Dodge Poetry Festival in Newark in October 2018, just two weeks before she died. Before our panel began, she got up from her chair and said: "I want to meet her," looking at me. Me? I looked behind me, thinking she was talking to someone else, but I was the only one on that stage. She smiled and said hello and shook my hand and said, "Hi, I'm Ntozake," and I felt embarrassed that I had not initiated the greeting, humbled and a little ashamed that she got up to welcome me instead. When I found my voice a beat or two later, it was quiet. I said, "I'm honored. Your work means everything to me, to all of us." By us, I meant our panel—ironically, about voice—which consisted of four Black women poets. We read our work and talked a bit about what silence and speech meant to us. The packed audience lined up to ask questions, mostly about how race and gender inform our work, and what those particular identities mean to us in terms of outspokenness and disclosure.

But one audience member asked—and yes, we all cringed, knowing the question was asked because we were all Black and all self-identified as women—if there were any *white* poets whose work we read and admired (emphasis: questioner's). We each named a few—Sharon Olds, Brigit Pegeen Kelly, and of course Muriel Rukeyser, a bisexual writer whose phrase from her poem "The Speed of Darkness"[1] gave us the title of our panel.

Shange's sole example, however, was Judy Grahn. In fact, according to Hilton Als's 2010 *New York Times* article about Shange, Grahn's poem "The Common Woman" inspired her iconic Tony Award–winning play, *for colored girls who have considered suicide / when the rainbow is enuf.*[2] I hadn't read or heard of Grahn's work before that mention at Dodge, and I remember looking up "The Common Woman" later and feeling not a little outrage about that lapse in my education. But it feels right to help rectify that in the process of writing this essay, in conversation with this particular memory of Ntozake Shange and her work, and my own lived experience as a Black non-Lesbian cisgender woman writer.

Let me say it plainly: I owe my initial and ongoing independence from, and critical language about, non-patriarchal theory and creative practice to the work of Lesbian writers and thinkers, full stop. Audre Lorde, first and forever; I also name Radclyffe Hall, Adrienne Rich, June Jordan, Alice Walker, Rita Mae Brown, Gloria Anzaldúa, Jeanette Winterson, Pauli Murray; two of my teachers, Carol Potter and Sappho scholar Eloise Klein Healy; and younger writers, my colleagues and peers—Bettina Judd, Alexis Pauline Gumbs, Dawn Lundy Martin, Anastacia Renée, and Lauren K. Alleyne, to name just five.

I now add Judy Grahn to that esteemed gathering of influences. I love the accessibility of her writing, the story quality steeped in both deep research and richly lived experience—a balance that strikes me as simply *true*. On an elemental level, in *The Highest Apple* I connect to the openness apparent in Grahn's thinking, her wide-ranging curiosity and consistent commitment to Lesbian and Queer communities—a commitment built upon acknowledgment and respect for one another's total wellbeing as a set of ongoing actions. Those actions, based upon the idea of commonality—"we get to belong to a number of overlapping groups, not just one," Grahn articulates (131)[3]—are not in service to power or profit, but to that wellbeing itself, on both individual and collective levels in parallel.

To that end, imagine my surprise reading in the introduction that she took inspiration for her early approach to building those communities from the Nation of Islam. She first heard Elijah Muhammad on the radio—more than a decade before I was born to parents who were active members of the Nation—and learned from his teachings to adapt for Lesbians the Black Muslims' message of "the essential importance of autonomy, self-determination, and community" (32). At a moment when xenophobia seems to be hitting new strident highs,[4] her theories about reframing origins resonates deeply. The *Highest Apple* shows us that we have so much in common with each other as human beings, especially when we begin to connect from a place of love and acceptance. We can build and evolve and create more powerfully when we recognize that. There is a generosity to that openness I mentioned earlier that cannot be overstated.

After our panel at Dodge, I spent a brief moment alone with Shange, kneeling down to take a selfie with her—for which she smiled freely and broadly—and to chat. She shared her laughter with me as we recalled my answer to another question from a white audience member, something like: "What if it's better to be silent, because the Bible says . . ." Slowly and patiently, so I could choose my words with care, I replied something like this, though I'm positive the original and exact words held more eloquence: "I've been silent for a long time, my voice stuffed down by the weight of fear and expectation. And now that I am free from that fear and have found my voice, I am going to use it." I said that last part slowly, with more than a little anger—feeling that the statement beneath the question was for us to *shut up*. I worried aloud that maybe I was too harsh, basically flipping that *shut up* right on back to the questioner. Shange, laughing, said: "I thought you were astounding."

I think women are astounding. Lesbians have been saying so from the beginning. I carry that knowledge and Shange's generous acknowledgment with me, and bring it forward as a teacher, hoping my students will surpass me and keep reaching up for the nurturing they need, and keep finding it in wild abundance, beyond any attempts by limiting beliefs and very real oppressions to silence, interrupt, and harm them. One path to that surpassing, which perhaps has for too long been missed on a larger scale: reading Judy Grahn. Here's hoping more of us find our way there sooner, never ignoring our common multivalence, our power to love and to make and to imagine.

Notes

1 "The Speed of Darkness," Muriel Rukeyser. Poetry Foundation, reprinted from *The Collected Poems of Muriel Rukeyser* (2006). https://www.poetryfoundation.org/poems/56287/the-speed-of-darkness.

2 Hilton Als, "Color Vision," *The New York Times*, November 1, 2010. https://www.newyorker.com/magazine/2010/11/08/color-vision.

3 Judy Grahn, *The Highest Apple*, Dover, FL: Sinister Wisdom, 2023.

4 Erika Lee, "Op-Ed: What Does It Mean to Be an American? Ask an Immigrant," *Los Angeles Times*, July 4, 2021. https://www.latimes.com/opinion/story/2021-07-04/immigrants-american-history-xenophobia-citizens.

Khadijah Queen is the author of six books of innovative poetry and hybrid prose, most recently Anodyne (Tin House 2020). Her verse play Non-Sequitur (Litmus Press 2015) won the Leslie Scalapino Award for Innovative Women's Performance Writing. With K. Ibura, she co-edited Infinite Constellations, (FC2 2023), a multi-genre anthology of speculative writing by authors from the global majority. Her book of literary theory and criticism, Radical Poetics, is forthcoming from University of Michigan Press.

NOTES

Introduction

1 Editors' Note: In the years since this original intro-duction was written, the reclaimed term "Queer" has come to operate in concert with, in opposition to, as syn-onym, as antonym, and as othernym for the phrase "Gay and Lesbian." With this understanding in mind, *Another Mother Tongue: Gay Words, Gay Worlds*, much like this text, may serve both the Gay and Lesbian canon and Queer can-on in ways that overlap and diverge.

2 Mary J. Carruthers, "The Re-Vision of the Muse: Adrienne Rich, Audre Lorde, Judy Grahn and Olga Brou-mas," *The Hudson Review* XXXVI, no. 2 (Summer 1983): 293–322.

I: A Heart-Shaped Journey to a Similar Place

1 Sappho, *Greek Lyric*, Vol. 1, trans. David A. Campbell (Cambridge, MA: Harvard University Press, 1982), 131. I appreciate the lovely interpretive translations of Sappho's work that have been done by Mary Barnard, Willis Barn-stone, Susie Q. Groden, and others I see occasionally. However, I could not have done the particular compari-sons in this book without a source that is simply a literal, word-for-word translation of Sappho's content. So I have used only one text for her words, David A. Campbell's *Greek Lyric*, for which I am completely grateful.

2   Information thanks to Audre Lorde.

3   Suzy Q. Groden, *The Poems of Sappho* (New York: Bobbs-Merrill Co., 1966), xi. "During her lifetime Lesbos was a state of political turmoil and when the commoner Pittacus came to power, Sappho and others of the aristocratic party may have been forced to leave the island to live as exiles in Sicily." Ann Forfreedom, who I heard give a talk on the subject in San Diego in the early 1970s, mentioned two exiles, and that Pittacus became a word meaning "tyrant."

4   David Robison, *Our Debt to Greece and Rome* (New York: Cooper Square, 1963), 25.

5   Elly Bulkin and Joan Larkin, eds., *Lesbian Poetry* (New York: The Gay Presses of New York, 1982).

6   I want to thank Robert Duncan for giving me this phrase.

7   John Boswell, *Christianity, Homosexuality, and Social Tolerance* (Chicago: University of Chicago Press, 1980), 220.

8   Kenneth Rexroth and Ling Chung, trans., in *Women Poets of the World*, ed. Joanna Bankier and Deidre Lashgari (New York: Macmillan, 1983), 24–25.

9   Paula Gunn Allen, *The Woman Who Owned the Shadows* (San Francisco: Spinsters Ink, 1983), 155–56.

10   Contrast Dickinson's isolation and dependence on her family with Walt Whitman's uneasy freedom, on the road, rootless. The one was bound to a room in her father's house and the unrequited disappointed love she could not have and would not give up; the other poet was bound to a rootless though magnificent road and lover after lover with whom he could not bond nor build permanent place.

In their individual ways, they were both isolated, both lived in fragmented, incompleted worlds, both were outcasts from their society because of their chosen arts as well as their chosen loves, and both are currently emerging as the most important American poets of the nineteenth century.

11 Adrienne Rich, *On Lies, Secrets, and Silence* (New York: W. W. Norton, 1979), 176. For several years, Rich lived just up the road from Dickinson's home in Amherst, Massachusetts.

12 Lillian Faderman, *Surpassing the Love of Men* (New York: William Morrow, 1981), 176.

13 Rebecca Patterson, *The Riddle of Emily Dickinson* (New York: Cooper Square, 1973). Patterson is of interest as the first person to point out the emotional attachments to women that are evident in Dickinson's work. But her painfully literal interpretations have become outdated by the more recent scholarship of Lillian Faderman, Paula Bennett, and others. I found Patterson valuable for the details of Kate Scott's Lesbian life and for actual versions of the poetry itself that are more entrancing to me than versions published in *The Complete Poems of Emily Dickinson*, ed. Thomas H, Johnson (Boston: Little Brown, 1951). According to Dickinson scholar Paula Bennett, although Scott and Dickinson had a tumultuous affair for two years, and Scott intermittently swirled like a disruptive whirlwind into Emily's life thereafter, Sue Gilbert Dickinson was the mainstay love of the poet's life. (Private conversation; thank you Paula Bennett.)

14 Ibid, p. 125. Johnson (Dickinson, 1951), op. cit., p. 312.) used the version "must be" to describe the north side of Emily's cottage.

15 Ibid, p. 226. Johnson has a different version ending "penury and home." Op. cit., p. 572.

16 Johnson, 382. It is the center of three verses.

17 Amy Lowell, *The Complete Poetical Works of Amy Lowell* (Boston: Houghton Mifflin, 1955), 212.

18 *The Penguin Book of Women Poets*, eds. Carol Cosman, Joan Keefe, and Kathleen Weaver (New York: Penguin Books, 1978), 331. A similar thought was expressed at about the same time by Elsa Gidlow, writing in 1919 of both the threat of the streets and of the Lesbian as a sinister, witchy robber:

> I have robbed the garrulous streets,
> Thieved a fair girl from their blight,
> I have stolen her for a sacrifice
> That I shall make to this night.
>
> I have brought her, laughing,
> To my quietly dreaming garden.
> For what shall be done there
> I ask no man pardon.

These two stanzas from "For the Goddess Too Well Known" is an early rendition of the Lesbian who rescues her lover from the oppression and "blight" of a masculine public world. This becomes a major theme for the work of literally dozens of Lesbian poets during the 1970s. The poem is in *Sapphic Songs* (Mill Valley, CA: Druid Heights, 1982) originally published as a collection in 1923.

19 Radclyffe Hall, *The Well of Loneliness* (New York: Avon Books, 1975).

20 Gertrude Stein, *The Yale Gertrude Stein*, ed. Richard Kostalanetz (New Haven: Yale University Press, 1980), xix.

21 Alice Dunbar Nelson, a woman-loving woman poet and contemporary of H.D.'s, also wrote extensively on

World War I. Her poem "I Sit and Sew" expresses frustration with women's relegation to domestic duties and inability to participate more directly in war efforts.

22 H.D., "Winter Love," *Hermetic Definition* (New York: New Directions, 1972), 97.

23 Judy Grahn, *The Work of a Common Woman* (Trumansburg: Crossing Press, 1984), 67.

24 Rita Mae Brown's *The Hand that Cradles the Rock* was published soon after (1972) on the East Coast. Elsa Gidlow, of course, had published overtly lesbian poetry in the 1920s.

25 Pat Parker, "from cavities of bones," *The Complete Works of Pat Parker* (Dover, FL: Sinister Wisdom, 2016), 53.

26 Paula Gunn Allen, "Beloved Women," in *Lesbian Poetry*, ed. Bulkin and Larkin, 65–67. Also "Beloved Women: Lesbians in American Indian Cultures," *Conditions* 7 (1981).

27 Interestingly, the poets who "came out" late in their careers, or who (in H.D.'s case) most severely covered the lesbian content of their work, are all women with children: H.D., Rich, Lorde, Allen. The others—Dickinson (who did not cover up the Lesbianism of her words—others did it for her), Lowell, Stein, myself, and Broumas—are all without children. Parker came out into a Lesbian-feminist movement that supported her adoption of her two children. Minnie Bruce Pratt wrote the definitive description of a mother losing custody of her children because of her lesbianism, in her 1990 book of poems, *Crime Against Nature*.

28 Audre Lorde, "Walking our Boundaries," *The Black Unicorn* (New York: W. W. Norton, 1978), 39.

29 "A Woman Is Talking to Death," *The Work of a Common Woman*, 113–31. Later, the subject of a bridge and the crossing over by Lesbians is treated caustically and personally in a complex poem by Los Angeles poet Eloise Klein Healy. Rigid movement politics ("Your fist and a finger always pointing") are seen as the villain that closed the dialogue of inter-cultural friendship; as with "A Woman Is Talking to Death," the bridge is the Bay Bridge, leading into San Francisco. The two women cannot reach the bridge, the poem says, because of an argument they are having on the on-ramp leading to it; they are separated by the argument, "a rope ladder suspended in cold green water." The poem ends with desire for reconciliation: "We're bulldogs both of us. I Give in. I want to give in. / I miss imagining you. / Questions and answers. / I miss each of us pointing out / something" (from "What Is Left of Our History," unpublished ms.).

30 Olga Broumas, *Beginning with O* (New Haven: Yale University Press, 1977), 62.

31 Audre Lorde, "October," *Chosen Poems, Old and New* (New York: W. W. Norton, 1982), 108. The poem was written in 1980.

32 Adrienne Rich, *The Dream of a Common Language* (New York: W. W. Norton, 1978), 34.

33 Ibid., 25.

34 Mary Carruthers refers to this as "eschatology."

35 Paula Gunn Allen, "Moonstream," *Skin and Bones* (San Francisco: Passion Press, 1985).

36 Adrienne Rich, "Twenty-One Love Poems," *The Dream of a Common Language* (New York: W. W. Norton, 1978), 35–36.

37 Judy Grahn, *The Queen of Wands* (Trumansburg: Crossing Press, 1983), 3–6.

38 Paula Gunn Allen, "Red Roots of White Feminism," in *Sinister Wisdom* no. 25 (Winter 1984): 34.

II: Writing from a House of Women

1 Sappho, *Greek Lyric*, Vol. 1, trans. David A. Campbell (Cambridge, MA: Harvard University Press, 1982), 147.

2 H.D., "The Wise Sappho," *Notes on Thought and Vision* (San Francisco: City Lights Books, 1982), 58–59.

3 Jean Gould, *Amy: The World of Amy Lowell and the Imagist Movement* (New York: Dodd, Mead and Co., 1975), 319.

4 I learned the basics of my writing as a child, especially from Edgar Allan Poe, Alfred Lord Tennyson, Alfred Noyes and other balladeers, John Donne, E.E. Cummings, and Gertrude Stein.

5 Amy Lowell, *The Complete Poetical Works of Amy Lowell*, (Boston: Houghton Mifflin, 1925), 443.

6 H.D., *Helen in Egypt* (New York: New Directions, 1961), 85.

7 *The Penguin Book of Homosexual Verse*, ed. Stephen Coote, (Suffolk, England: Penguin Books, 1983), 272–73.

8 Gertrude Stein, *The Yale Gertrude Stein*, ed. Richard Kostalanetz (New Haven: Yale University Press, 1980), 109.

9 Gertrude Stein, "Poetry and Grammar," *Lectures in America* (Boston: Beacon Hill, 1935), 236.

10 Paula Gunn Allen tells me that she believes it was Timothy Leary who first coined the phrase "culture trance." During the sixties he taught that it could be broken through the carefully controlled use of mind-altering drugs, especially LSD.

11 The poster was taken from Sappho, "Translation #2," *Sappho, A New Translation*, trans. Mary Barnard (Berkeley: University of California Press, 1958).

12 Pat Parker, "GROUP," *Movement in Black* (Trumansburg: Crossing Press, 1983), 136–138.

13 Adrienne Rich, "Power and Danger: Works of a Common Woman," *The Work of a Common Woman* (Trumansburg: Crossing Press, 1984), 17–18.

14 Adrienne Rich, *The Dream of a Common Language* (New York: W. W. Norton, 1978).

15 Olga Broumas, "with the clear plastic speculum," *Lesbian Poetry*, eds. Elly Bulkin and Joan Larkin (New York: The Gay Presses of NY, 1981), 211.

16 Olga Broumas, *Beginning with O* (New Haven: Yale University Press, 1977), 70.

17 Alice Bloch, "Six Years," *The Penguin Books of Homosexual Verse*, op. cit., 375.

18 Arlene Stiebel, "The Common Woman's Common Language: Poems of Rich and Grahn," unpublished ms., 2–3.

19 Mary Carruthers, "The Re-Visioning of the Muse: Adrienne Rich, Audre Lorde, Judy Grahn, Olga Broumas," *The Hudson Review* XXXVI, no. 2 (Summer 1983): 293–322.

20 Audre Lorde, "Meet," *The Black Unicorn* (New York: W. W. Norton, 1978), 33–34.

21 Audre Lorde, *Chosen Poems, Old and New* (New York: W. W. Norton, 1982), 349.

22 Paula Gunn Allen, *Shadow Country* (University of California, Los Angeles, 1982), 132–36.

23 Judy Grahn, *The Queen of Wands* (Trumansburg, New York: Crossing Press, 1982), 22.

24 Pat Parker, *The Complete Works of Pat Parker* (Dover, FL: Sinister Wisdom, 2016), 29–39.

25   Adrienne Rich, "Readings of History," Collected Poems (New York: W. W. Norton, 2016), 133.

26   Adrienne Rich, "Split at the Root: An Essay on Jewish Identity (1982)," Blood, Bread, and Poetry: Selected Prose, 1979-1985 (New York: W. W. Norton, 1986), 100.

27   Adrienne Rich, "Notes toward a Politics of Location," Blood, Bread, and Poetry: Selected Prose, 1979-1985 (New York: W. W. Norton, 1986), 215.

28   Adrienne Rich, "Split at the Root," 122.

29   Ibid., 123.

30   Judy Grahn, love belongs to those who do the feeling (Los Angeles, CA: Red Hen Press, 2008), 40.

31   Audre Lorde, Collected Poems (New York: W. W. Norton, 2000), 493.

32   Ibid., 244.

33   A "House of Women" who call themselves "Africa" is described at length in Donna Allegra's poem "When People Ask," in Lesbian Poetry, eds. Bulkin and Larkin, 257: "say you are Africa come calling . . . a house of sisters sat up telling each other."

34   Paula Gunn Allen, "Some Like Indians Endure," Skins and Bones (San Francisco: Passion Press, 1985).

35   Paula Gunn Allen, "Grandmother," Coyote's Daylight Trip (Albuquerque: La Confluencia, 1978), 50.

36   Audre Lorde, Zami: A New Spelling of My Name (Trumansburg: Crossing Press, 1983).

III: To Surface with Lesbian Gods

1   Sappho, Greek Lyric, Vol. 1, trans. David A. Campbell (Cambridge: Harvard University Press, 1982), 131.

2   Judy Grahn, "Sashay Down the Lavender Trail," Another Mother Tongue (Boston: Beacon Press, 1984), 1–19.

3 Emily Dickinson, *The Complete Poems of Emily Dickinson*, ed. Thomas H. Johnson (Boston: Little Brown, 1951), 109.

4 The Seth Material is a collection of texts supposedly transmitted to Jane Roberts from a channeled spirit entity named Seth from 1963 to 1984. This body of texts was foundational to the New Age philosophical movement.

5 Amy Lowell, "Mise en Scene," *The Complete Poetical Works of Amy Lowell* (Boston: Houghton Mifflin, 1955), 210. Originally published in *Pictures of a Floating World*.

6 H.D., "The Walls Do Not Fall," *Selected Poems of H.D.* (New York: Grove Press, 1957), 79.

7 H.D., "Amaranth," *H.D.: Collected Poems 1912–1944* (New York: New Directions, 1983), 310–15. Louis Martz, for example, has discovered that H.D. masked three important poems about her disintegrating relationship with Aldington ("Amaranth," "Eros," and "Envy," not published in their original form until *Collected Poems 1912–1944*) as expansions of fragments of Sappho. "H.D.," Poetry Foundation, https://www.poetryfoundation.org/poets/h-d, accessed December 28, 2022.

8 H.D., *Notes on Thought and Vision* (San Francisco: City Lights Books, 1982), 21–22.

9 Of course, people of all genders may or may not have wombs. H.D. might argue that we all have access to wombmind consciousness regardless of gender or physical embodiment, and her contemporary, lesbian writer Djuna Barnes, makes essentially this argument in her groundbreaking novel *Nightwood*.

10 By which she means all people.

11 Allen, *Skins and Bones*. Originally published in *Feminary* vol. 13: 6.

12 Audre Lorde, *Chosen Poems, Old and New* (New York: W. W. Norton, 1982), 48.

13 Joy Harjo, "Moonlight," *She Had Some Horses* (New York: Thunder's Mouth Press, 1983), 51:

> "I know when the sun is in China
> because the night shining other-light
> crawls into my bed. She is the moon.
> Her eyes slit and yellow she is the last
> one out of a dingy bar in Albuquerque –
> Fourth Street or from similar avenues
> In Hong Kong. Where someone else has also
> awakened, the night thrown back and asked,
> 'Where is the moon, my lover?'
> And from here I always answer in my dreaming,
> 'the last time I saw her was in the arms
> of another sky.'"

14 Audre Lorde, *The Black Unicorn* (New York: W. W. Norton, 1978), 12.

15 Olga Broumas, *Beginning with O* (New Haven: Yale University Press, 1977), 7–8.

16 Mary Carruthers, "The Re-Visioning of the Muse: Adrienne Rich, Audre Lorde, Judy Grahn, Olga Broumas," *The Hudson Review* XXXVI, no. 2 (Summer 1983): 308–309.

17 Olga Broumas, *Pastoral Jazz* (Port Townsend: Copper Canyon Press, 1983), 21.

18 Adrienne Rich, *The Dream of a Common Language* (New York: W. W. Norton, 1978), 42.

19 Adrienne Rich, *Sources* (Woodside: Heyeck Press, 1983), 31.

20 Judy Grahn, "She Who," *The Work of a Common Woman* (Trumansburg: Crossing Press, 1984), 157.

21   Judy Grahn, *The Queen of Wands* (Trumansburg: Crossing Press, 1982), 88–89.

22   Judy Grahn, *The Queen of Swords* (Boston, MA: Beacon Press, 1987), 50-51.

23   Paula Gunn Allen, private conversation.

24   Paula Gunn Allen, *Shadow Country* (Los Angeles: University of California, 1982), 123–4.

25   Paula Gunn Allen, "Transitions," *Skins and Bones* (San Francisco: Passion Press, 1985).

26   Starhawk, "Consciousness, Politics and Magic," *The Politics of Women's Spirituality*, ed. Charlene Spretnak (New York: Doubleday, 1982), 177.

27   H.D.'s student, poet Robert Duncan, says she made the distinction very clear to him, that the "white island" is not Lesbianism itself. From a private conversation.

28   Carruthers, "The Re-Visioning of the Muse," 305.

29   Sappho, *Greek Lyrics*, 57: "from the shimmering leaves the sleep of enchantment comes down." She is describing the apple orchard they keep especially for Aphrodite while inviting her to it.

30   Audre Lorde, "Uses of the Erotic: The Erotic as Power," *Sister Outsider* (Trumansburg: Crossing Press, 1984), 53–59.

31   John J. Winkler, classics scholar who has studied Sappho's work extensively, pointed out to me that the word translated as "fellow-fighter," and used by Sappho to describe the kind of relationship she desired from Aphrodite, is a Greek word of male bonding, male companions-in-arms, who were, generally speaking, also lovers. Private conversation.

BIBLIOGRAPHY

Allen, Paula Gunn. *Skins and Bones*. San Francisco: Passion Press, 1985.

——"Red Roots of White Feminism." *Sinister Wisdom* no. 25 (Spring 1984): 34–46.

—— *The Women Who Owned the Shadows*. San Francisco: Spinsters Ink, 1983.

—— *Shadow Country*. Los Angeles: University of California, American Indian Studies Center, 1982.

—— "Beloved Women: The Lesbian in American Indian Culture." *Conditions* 7 (1981): 65–87.

—— "The Sacred Hoop: A Contemporary Indian Perspective on American Indian Literature." In *Literature of the American Indian: Views and Interpretations*, edited by Abraham Chapman, 111–136. New York: New American Library, 1975.

Bankier, Joanna and Deirdre Lashgari, eds. *Women Poets of the World*. New York: Macmillan Publishing Co., 1983.

Bogin, Meg. *The Women Troubadours*. Scarborough, England: Paddington Press, Ltd., 1976.

Boswell, John. *Christianity, Social Tolerance, and Homosexuality*. Chicago: University of Chicago Press, 1980.

Broumas, Olga. *Pastoral Jazz*. Townsend, WA: Copper Canyon, 1983.

—— *Beginning With O*. New Haven: Yale University Press, 1977.

—— Unpublished prose ms.

Bulkin, Elly and Joan Larkin, eds. *Lesbian Poetry*. New York: Gay Presses of New York, 1985.

Cameron, Anne. *Daughters of Copper Woman*. Vancouver, BC: Press Gang, 1981.

Carruthers, Mary J. "Adrienne Rich's 'Sources.'" *River Styx* no. 15 (1984).

———— "The Re-Vision of the Muse: Adrienne Rich, Audre Lorde, Judy Grahn, Olga Broumas." *The Hudson Review* (Summer 1983).

Coote, Stephen, ed. *The Penguin Book of Homosexual Verse*. Suffolk, England: Penguin, 1983.

Daly, Mary. *Gyn/Ecology: The Metaethics of Radical Feminism*. Boston: Beacon Press, 1978.

———— *Pure Lust*. Boston: Beacon Press, 1984.

Davis, Elizabeth Gould. *The First Sex*. New York: GP Putnam's Sons, 1971.

Dickinson, Emily. *The Complete Poems of Emily Dickinson*, edited by Thomas H. Johnson. Boston: Little Brown & Co., 1951.

———— *Selected Poems and Letters of Emily Dickinson*, edited by Robert N. Linscott. New York: Doubleday, 1959.

Faderman, Lillian. *Surpassing the Love of Men*. New York: William Morrow and Company, 1981.

Gidlow, Elsa. *Sapphic Songs: Eighteen to Eighty*. Mill Valley, CA: Druid Heights Books, 1982.

Gould, Jean. *Amy: The World of Amy Lowell and the Imagist Movement*. New York: Dodd, Mead & Co. 1975.

Grahn, Judy. *love belongs to those who do the feeling*. Los Angeles, CA: Red Hen Press, 2008.

———— *The Work of a Common Woman*. Trumansburg, NY: Crossing Press, 1984. Originally published in 1978. A collection consisting of "The Common Women

Poems" (1969), "She Who" (written in 1972), "A Woman Is Talking to Death (1974), and "Confrontations with the Devil in the Form of Love" (written in 1977).

―――― *Another Mother Tongue: Gay Words, Gay Worlds.* Boston: Beacon Press, 1984.

――, *The Queen of Swords.* Included in *The Judy Grahn Reader*, San Francisco: Aunt Lute Press, 2009; Boston: Beacon Press, 1987, 1988.

―――― *The Queen of Wands.* Trumansburg, NY: Crossing Press, 1982.

Guest, Barbara. *Herself Defined.* New York: Doubleday, 1984.

Harjo, Joy. *She Had Some Horses.* New York: Thunder's Mouth, 1983.

Harrison, Jane Ellen. *Epilegomena to the Study of Greek Religion and Themis.* New York: University Books, 1962.

―――― *Mythology.* New York: Harcourt, Brace and World, Inc., 1924.

H.D. *Collected Poems, 1912–1944.* New York: New Directions, 1983.

―――― *Bid Me to Live.* New York: Dial, 1983.

―――― *Notes on Thought and Vision.* San Francisco: City Lights Books, 1982. (Includes "The Wise Sappho," an essay.)

―――― *Trilogy.* New York: New Directions Press, 1973.

―――― *Helen in Egypt.* New York: New Directions, 1961.

―――― *Hermetic Definition.* New York: New Directions, 1958.

―――― *Selected Poems of H.D.* New York: Grove Press, 1957.

————— Collected Poems of H.D. New York: Liveright Publishing Co., 1925.

Lorde, Audre. Collected Poems. New York: W. W. Norton, 2000.

————— Sister Outsider. Trumansburg, NY: Crossing Press, 1984.

————— Chosen Poems – Old and New. New York: W. W. Norton, 1982.

————— Zami, A New Spelling of My Name. Trumansburg, NY: Crossing Press, 1982.

————— The Black Unicorn. New York: W. W. Norton, 1978.

————— "The Master's Tools Will Never Dismantle the Master's House." This Bridge Called My Back (Watertown, MA: Persephone Press, 1981), 98-101.

Lowell, Amy. The Complete Poetical Works of Amy Lowell. Boston: Houghton Mifflin, 1955.

————— Pictures of the Floating World. Boston: Houghton Mifflin, 1924.

Marks, Elaine. "Lesbian Intertextuality." In Homosexuals and French Literature, Cultural Contexts/Critical Texts, edited by George Stambolian and Elaine Marks. Ithaca, NY: Cornell University Press, 1979.

Ostriker, Alicia. Writing like a Woman. Ann Arbor: University of Michigan Press, 1983.

Parker, Pat. The Complete Works of Pat Parker. Dover, FL: Sinister Wisdom, 2016.

————— Movement in Black. Trumansburg, NY: Crossing Press, 1983. (First published in 1978.)

———, Sister Love: The Letters of Audre Lorde and Pat Parker 1975-1989. Dover, FL: Sinister Wisdom 2018.

Patterson, Rebecca. The Riddle of Emily Dickinson. New York: Houghton Mifflin, 1951.

Neumann, Erich. *The Great Mother*. Princeton, NJ: Princeton University Press, 1963.

Rich, Adrienne. *Collected Poems: 1950-2012*. New York: W. W. Norton, 2016.

—— Blood, Bread, and Poetry: Selected Prose 1979-1985. New York: W. W. Norton, 1986.

—— *Sources*. Woodside, CA: Heyeck Press, 1983.

—— *A Wild Patience Has Taken Me this Far*. New York: W. W. Norton, 1983.

—— *On Lies, Secrets and Silence. Selected Prose, 1966–1978*. New York: W. W. Norton, 1979. Especially "Vesuvius at Home: The Power of Emily Dickinson" (1975) and "Power and Danger: Works of a Common Woman" (1977).

—— *The Dream of a Common Language: Poems 1974–1977*. New York: W. W. Norton, 1978.

—— *Of Woman Born*. New York: W. W. Norton, 1977.

—— *Adrienne Rich's Poetry*, edited by Barbara Harlesworth Gelpi and Albert Gelpi. New York: W. W. Norton, 1975.

—— *Diving Into the Wreck*. New York: W. W. Norton, 1973.

Robinson, Janice S. *H.D.: The Life and Work of an American Poet*. Boston: Houghton Mifflin, 1982.

Rothery, Guy Cadogan. *The Amazons in Antiquity and Modern Times*. London: Frances Griffiths, 1910.

Sappho. *Greek Lyric*, Vol 1. Translated by David A. Campbell. Cambridge, MA: Harvard University Press, 1982.

—— *The Poems of Sappho*. Translated by Suzie Q. Groden. New York: Bobbs-Merrill, 1966.

———— *Sappho: A New Translation*. Translated by Mary Barnard. Berkeley: University of California Press, 1958.

Sewall, Richard B. *The Life of Emily Dickinson*. New York: Farrar, Straus and Giroux, 1980.

Sobol, Donald. *The Amazons of Greek Mythology*. South Brunswick: A. S. Barnes, 1972.

Spretnak, Charlene, ed. *The Politics of Women's Spirituality*. Garden City, NY: Doubleday, 1982.

Starhawk. "Consciousness, Politics and Magic." In *The Politics of Women's Spirituality*, edited by Charlene Spretnak, 177-189. New York: Doubleday, 1982.

Stein, Gertrude. *Fernhurst, Q. E. D. and Other Early Writings*. New York: Liveright, 1983.

———— *The Yale Gertrude Stein*. New Haven: Yale University Press, 1980.

———— *A Primer for the Gradual Understanding of Gertrude Stein*. Los Angeles: Black Sparrow Press, 1971.

———— *Letters in America*. Boston: Beacon Hill, 1935.

Stiebel, Arlene. "The Common Woman's Common Language: Poems of Rich and Grahn." Unpublished paper.

Winkler, John J. Three lectures on Sappho delivered at New College of California, San Francisco, Fall 1983.

ACKNOWLEDGMENTS

My thanks to Mary Carruthers for her crisp mind and definition of "Lesbian Poetry"; to Paula Gunn Allen as always for hours of exhilarating conversation, definitions of metaphysics and Hermeticism, for giving me access to her library of spiritual traditions, and for teaching a course in comparative spiritualities; to Judith McDaniel for sending her precious copy of *Pictures of the Floating World*; to Adrienne Rich for a ms. copy of *Sources* and for wonderful praises as I went along; to Olga Broumas for generously sending ms. material; to Pat Parker for being a poet-comrade-in-arms in those early days when the going was really rough; to Sherry Thomas for loving belief in the ideas behind the work and for firm editorial guidance; to Karen Sjoholm for her friendship.

Thanks also to Betty De Shong Meador for responding to the ideas of this book with a woman-based Jungian perspective. For supporting me (literally as well as psychologically) I am grateful to Beverly Tannenhaus and Katharyn Aal of the Women Writers Workshop and to Rita Speicher and Rachel DeVries of the (former) Women's Writers Center, both located in New York state.

I especially want to express appreciation to Duncan McNaughton, Diane DiPrima, Robert Duncan, David Meltzer, Louis Patler, and Michael Palmer of the New College Poetics program for their support of this project—John J. Winkler for his "many-minded" lectures on Sappho;

Duncan for hiring me to deliver three lectures on Sappho to his class; Diane for saying, when I said, "Oh, I can't do that," "Oh, of course you can." I just want to thank Diane for so often being there, ahead of me, and making a way for me.

This edition, thirty-eight years after the first, is only possible because of the vision and persistent effort of Julie Enszer, and I thank her from the bottom of my heart. By her invitation two younger editors, Alicia Mountain and Alyse Knorr, brought the manuscript more up to date. With Julie's wise guidance, six younger people contributed their comments, insights, personal stories, invaluable critiques, and always welcome praises. I thank them all. I thank my spouse Kris Brandenburger, for setting me up with everything I need to keep working, and for being my best advisor.